PUZZLEGRAMS

A colourful collection of classic puzzles designed by Pentagram

Books UK Ltd.

This edition published in 1993 by
Books UK Limited by arrangement with
Ebury Press, an imprint of Random House UK
20 Vauxhall Bridge Road, London SW1V 2SA

British Library Cataloguing in Publication Data
Pentagram Design
Puzzlegrams, a collection of puzzles in pictures
I. Pictorial puzzles — Collections
793.73

ISBN 0 09 1781566

Printed in Singapore

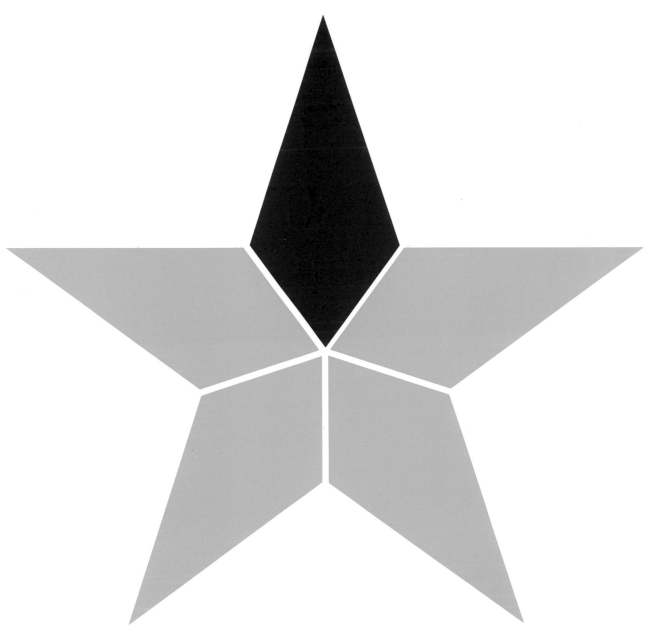

A novelty toy in the shape of a pentagram is made from five leaves of coloured plastic, each yellow on one side and blue on the other. In the standard model, the leaves are all the same way up so that the pentagram formed is all-yellow on the first side and all-blue on the second. This is a variant which has one leaf reversed. From one side it appears to have four yellow leaves and one blue: from the other, four blue and one yellow. By reversing different combinations of leaves, what is the total number of distinguishable pentagrams that can be made?

Place a coin on any point of the star and slide it along a straight line to another point. Place a second coin on any vacant point and similarly slide it along a line to reach another open point. Continue in the same manner until seven coins have been placed on seven points, leaving only one vacant point.

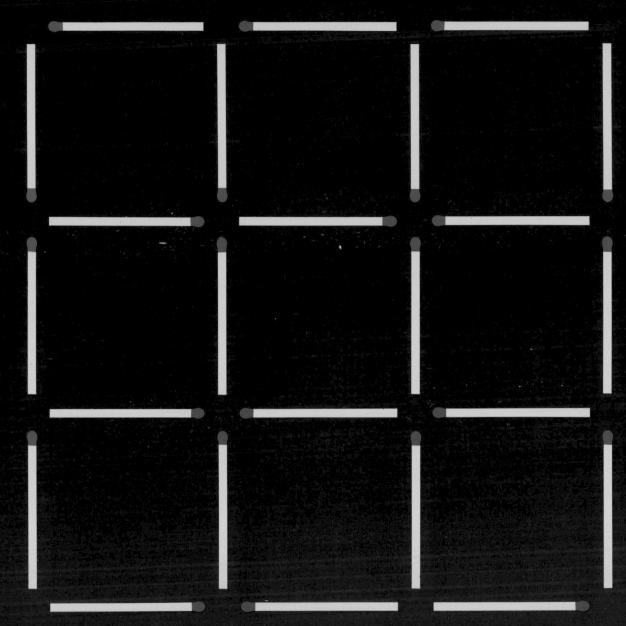

Remove eight matches from the twenty-four so as to leave just two squares, which should not touch.

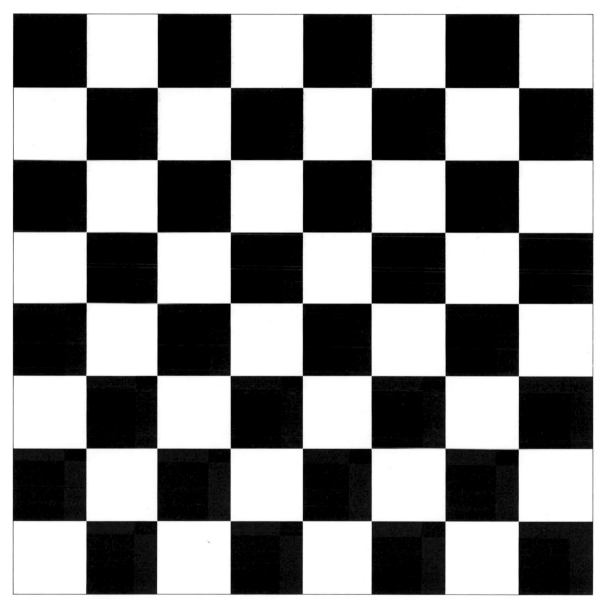

How many squares are on
a chess board?

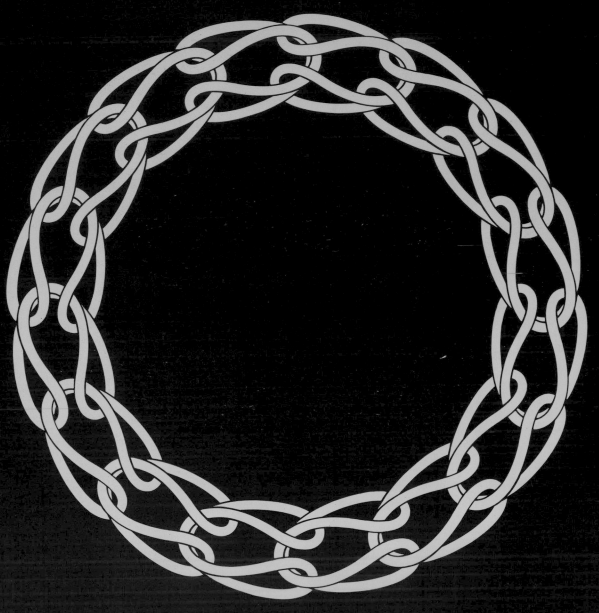

A jeweller needs to separate this
necklace into its individual links
while damaging it as little as
possible. What is the smallest
number of links which need to
be cut to achieve this?

Divide the circle into four areas
the same shape and size, each
containing two stars.

A man walking his dog along a straight country track spots a friend in the distance. They wave to one another, and the dog sprints ahead to greet her. As soon as it arrives, the dog turns round and runs straight back, then turns again and runs back to the girl, who is by now nearer. The dog continues running in this way until the two meet. Given that they are initially a mile apart, and each walks at a steady speed of three miles an hour, and the dog runs at nine miles an hour, how many trips did the dog make, and what total distance did he cover?

One-fifth of a hive of bees flew to the ladamba flower, one-third to the slandbara, and three times the difference of these two numbers flew to an arbor. One bee continued to fly about, attracted by the fragrant ketaki and the malati. What was the number of the bees?

If this symmetrical construction
hangs suspended, how many
cube faces would be exposed?

A prison guard ran his prison in accordance with certain security precautions which dictated that:
a) There must be twice as many prisoners on the top floor as on the ground floor,
b) No cell could be unoccupied,

c) There must always be eleven prisoners in the six cells on each of the four sides.
One night, nine prisoners escaped. Yet the next morning, when the warden made his rounds, nothing seemed amiss.

How many prisoners were there to begin with? How did the remaining prisoners rearrange themselves to conceal the escape?

Draw this figure without taking
the pen off the paper.

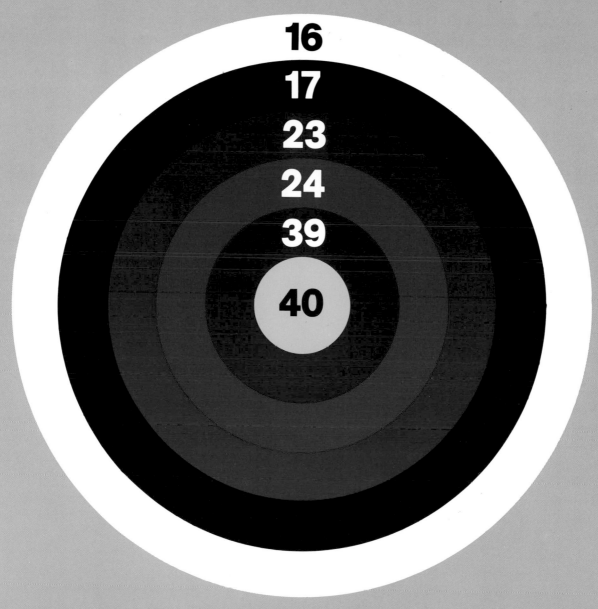

16
17
23
24
39
40

How many arrows are needed
to score exactly one hundred on
this target?

Five missionaries are on one bank of a river and five cannibals are on the other. The only method of crossing is by canoe and only one missionary and one cannibal can paddle.

The boat can hold three men. The missionaries do not trust the cannibals, and are unwilling to be outnumbered either in the boat or on either shore for the time it takes the boat to cross. What is more, the cannibals feel exactly the same way about the missionaries! Is it possible for both groups to cross safely?

13

An animal lover has seven pets.
Some are cats, the rest are dogs.
Each dog eats five biscuits and
each cat four biscuits. Thirty-
two biscuits in all are eaten.
How many dogs and how many
cats are there?

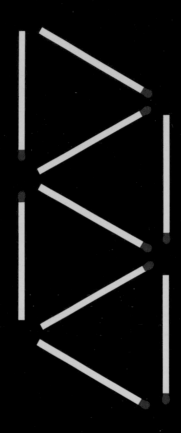

Make four triangles, all the
same size as the ones shown,
with only six matches.

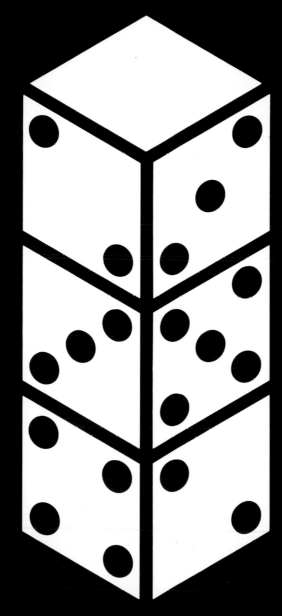

What are the numbers on the
top and base surface of this
stack of dice?

O T T

F F S

S

Reading from left to right can
you supply the next two letters
of this simple mnemonic?

I went to the wardrobe while my sister was asleep, so I left the light off. I found my shoes and socks, but they were in no kind of order – just a jumbled pile of six shoes of three brands, and a heap of twenty-four socks, black and brown. How many shoes and socks did I have to take to be sure I had a pair of matching shoes and a pair of matching socks?

A man ate one hundred grapes in
five days, each day eating six more
than on the previous day. How many
grapes did he eat on the first day?

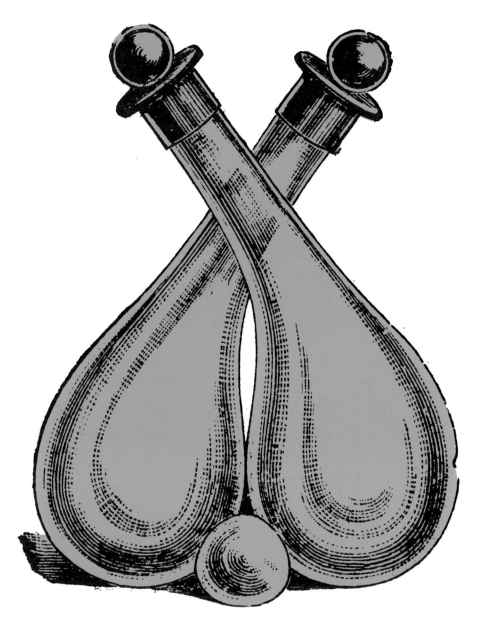

In the course of making a salad dressing, a glass of oil is placed next to a glass of vinegar. Someone takes a spoonful of vinegar and stirs it into the oil. Then a spoonful is taken from the oil glass and returned to the vinegar glass. At the end of this operation, which of the two glasses is the more contaminated?

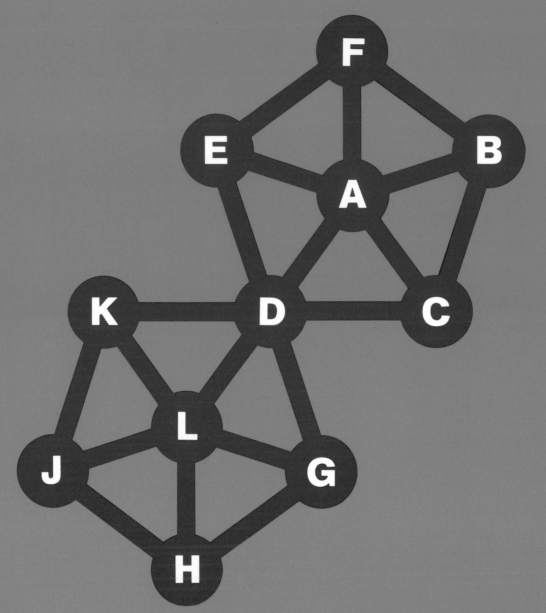

The floor plan of a building consists of two connected pentagons. Each of the inner corridors (AC, AD etc) is exactly one hundred feet long but, because of the pentagonal shape, each of the outer corridors (BC, CD etc) is one hundred and sixteen feet long. What is the shortest distance you would have to walk in order to pass along all corridors at least once?

A jig-saw contains one hundred pieces. A move consists of joining two clusters, including clusters of just one piece.

What is the minimum number of moves required to complete the puzzle?

Three spies, suspected as double agents, speak as follows when questioned:
Albert: 'Bertie is a mole'.
Bertie: 'Cedric is a mole'.
Cedric: 'Bertie is lying'.

Assuming that moles lie, other agents tell the truth, and there is just one mole among the three, who is he? If on the other hand there are two moles present, who are they?

If eight men can dig sixteen holes
in thirty-two days, how long
will it take four men to dig eight
holes of the same size?

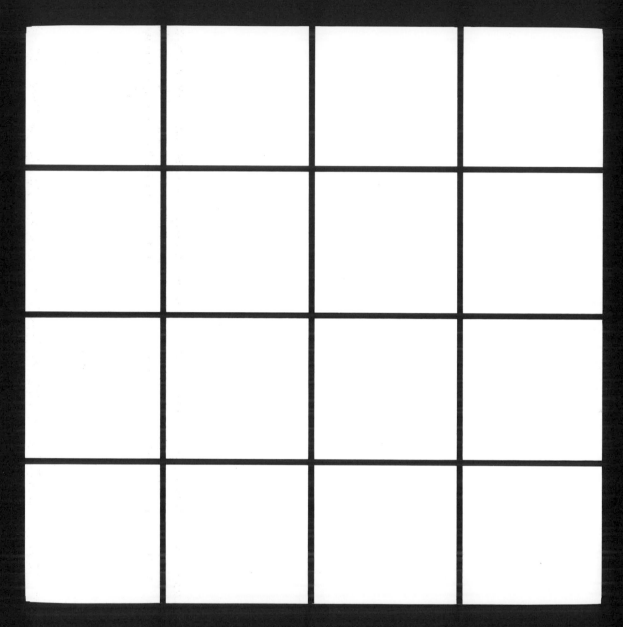

In this grid, colour four squares blue, three red, three green, three yellow and three white. Arrange them so that no two of the same colour are in line vertically, horizontally or diagonally.

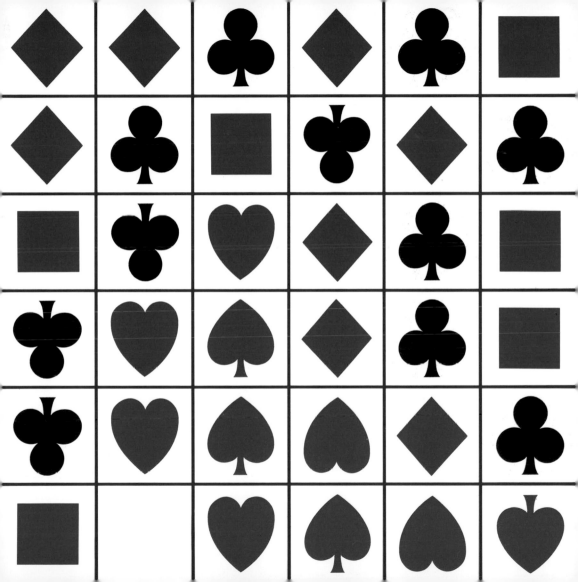

A bottle of beer costs £3. The beer
is worth £2 more than the bottle.
How much is the bottle worth?

Every afternoon during the school holidays, Klaus takes the tramcar either south to the airport to watch the jumbos take off, or north to the harbour to see the big ships come in. So as not to waste time, after he arrives at the tramstop he takes the first tram that arrives. Since north and south bound trams are equally frequent and his time of arrival at the tramstop is random, he reckons this should average out to the same number of afternoons at the harbour as at the airport. Yet at the end of the long summer vacation, sixty days, he finds he has been to the harbour fifty times, and the airport only ten. It is no coincidence. What could the explanation be?

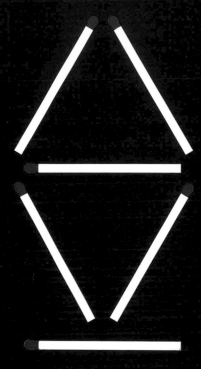

Rearrange three matches to make
eight equilateral triangles.

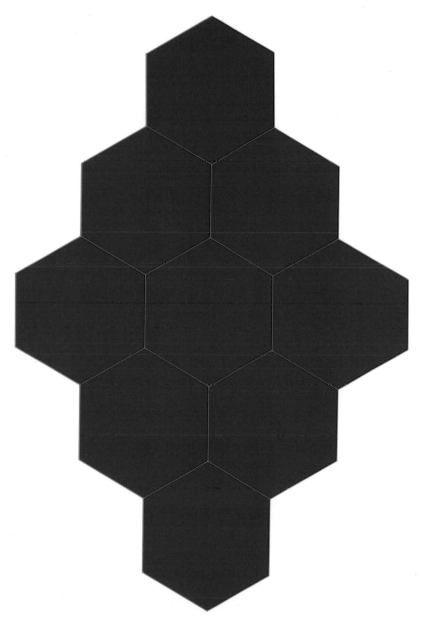

Place the digits 1 to 9 in the nine hexagons so that the total of the digits in the hexagons adjacent to any given hexagon is a multiple of the digit in the given hexagon.

Gordon, Stanley and Bobby are, not necessarily in that order, the striker, defender and goalkeeper in a local football team. The goalkeeper, who is the shortest of the three, is a bachelor. Gordon, who is Stanley's father-in-law, is taller than the defender. Who plays in which position?

Matthew, Mark and Luke live in the same block of flats, and work in the same office block. Every morning they set off to cycle to work together. After a month they realise that Matthew has arrived before Mark more often than after him and that Mark has arrived before Luke more often than after him. Is it possible that Luke has arrived before Matthew more often than after him?

Arrange the numbers from
thirty to fifty-four in the white
boxes, so that each row and
column adds up to one hundred
and fifty, and the main diagonals
add up to three hundred.

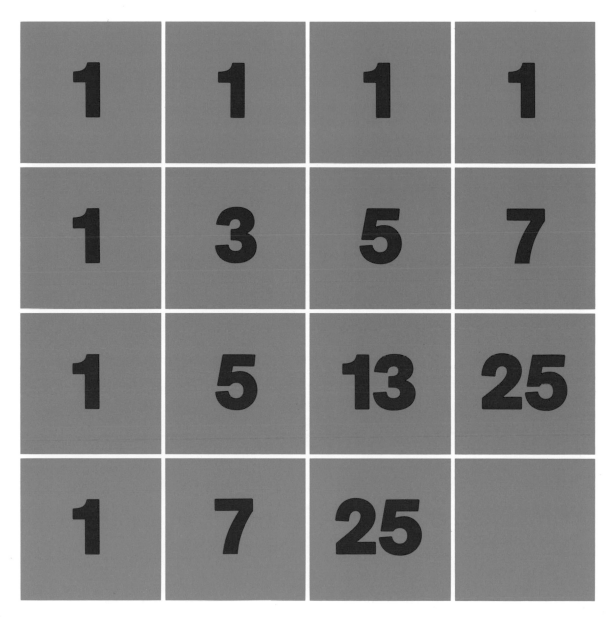

Complete the square logically.

In this simple arithmetic problem each numeral has been coded to the alphabet and replaced by a letter. What is the answer in figures?

This two cube calendar numerically
represents every day in a month.
What are the four digits that
cannot be seen on the left cube
and the three on the right?

During a fair, Nelson's column was wreathed with a garland. Assuming the column is an absolutely cylindrical shaft, sixty metres high, nine metres circumference, and the spiral garland passes around exactly five times, how would you find the length of the garland?

What is the minimum number of colours required to distinguish one county from another, providing no two adjoining counties are given the same colour?

Is it possible to draw this design in
one continuous movement without

Allow yourself fifty seconds to memorise as many of these items as possible. Then take two minutes to write down as many as you can remember.

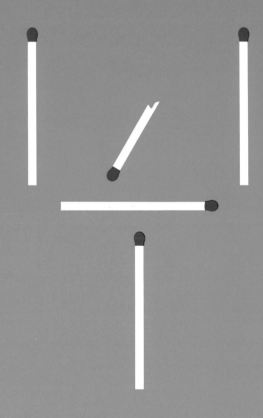

Rearrange two matches so that
the olive ends up outside the
glass but the glass retains exactly
the same shape.

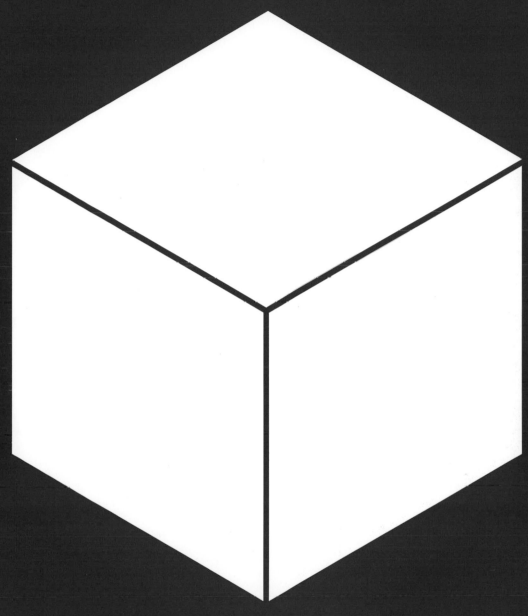

In how many distinguishably different ways is it possible to colour the faces of a white cube black?

A rabbit is trapped in the bottom right-hand corner of the maze. His only escape is via the exit at the top left-hand corner. There are one hundred and forty-five doors: nine shown by solid bars

are locked. Each locked door will open if the rabbit first passes through exactly eight open doors. It does not have to pass through every open door, but it must pass through every cell and all nine

locked doors. If it enters a cell or goes through a door a second time, the door will shut and the rabbit will be trapped. Find the rabbit's escape route.

Divide the plot into four pieces of equal size and shape with the same number of trees in each piece.

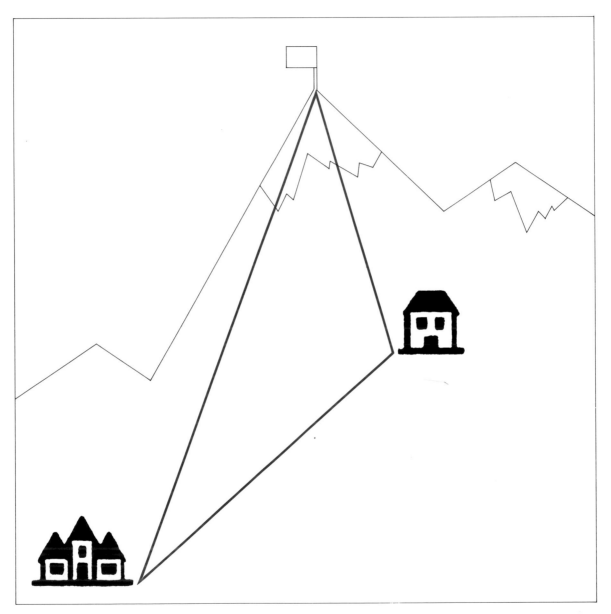

A mountaineer sets out from his hotel early one morning and climbs all day. Just as it is getting dark he reaches a hut at the foot of the main peak. He spends the night there. The next day he climbs to the top of the peak and then comes all the way down. He reaches his hotel just as it is getting dark. Is it possible that on both the first and second day he could have found himself at exactly the same height at the same time?

An explorer walks one mile due
south, turns and walks one mile
due east, turns again and walks
one mile due north. He finds
himself back where he started.
He shoots a bear. What colour is
the bear?

These identical drawings are views of an irregular three-dimensional object. The top drawing is a plan view looking down on the object, the second is looking at a side. What form does this object take?

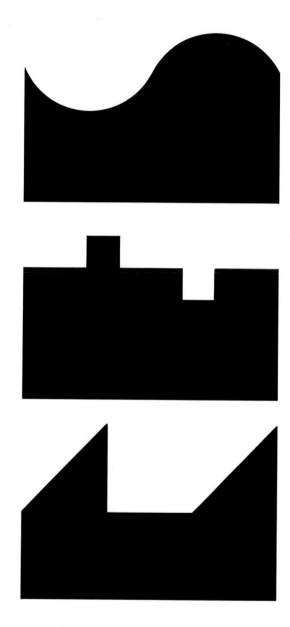

Cut each of these shapes into two pieces that are equal in size, shape and area, in other words so that the two halves could be placed exactly on top of one another. What do the three pairs of halves look like?

Cut a cross into the fewest
number of pieces which, when
rearranged, will fit together to
form two smaller crosses of
identical size.

Cut this symbol into four parts so
that the pieces can be arranged
to form a square.

A family gathering consists of father, mother, son, daughter, brother, sister, cousin, nephew, niece, uncle and aunt. But there are only two men and two women present. They have a common ancestor, and there has been no consanguine marriage. Explain how this is possible.

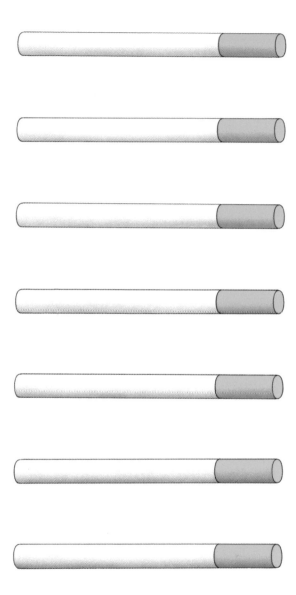

Rearrange these cigarettes so that each one touches the other six. The cigarettes cannot be bent or broken.

With a seven-minute hourglass
and an eleven-minute hourglass,
what is the quickest way to
time the boiling of an egg for
fifteen minutes?

If seven of the twelve edges of a hollow cube are cut as shown, and the faces then opened out, the result would be a cross shape as shown. Cutting different choices of edges will produce other shapes. How many different, continuous flat shapes can be created by cutting the edges of such a hollow cube? Two shapes are distinguishable if, when rotated or turned over, they still cannot be made to match.

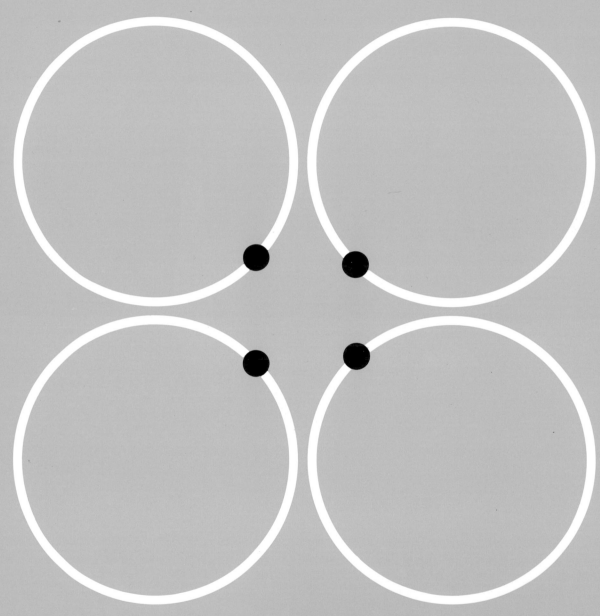

Four cyclists do their act on circular paths, each one third of a mile long. They start simultaneously at the black spots, with speeds of six, nine, twelve and fifteen miles per hour.

By the end of the act, after twenty minutes, how many times will they have simultaneously returned to the spots where they started?

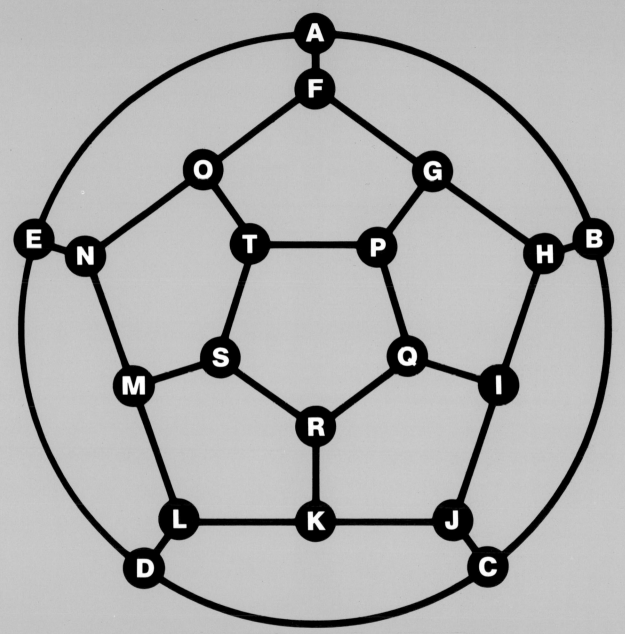

Here is a sketch map showing the only available roads in Problemania. Starting from A one morning, a man did a round tour of the country, spending a night in each town and returning to A on the twentieth day, having visited each town once and once only. The day he set out from A, a friend left from B, on the same sort of tour. He of course, finished up back at B. The fifth night of their tours they spent together at L, and the following night they again found themselves together in another town. At what other towns (if any) did they spend the night together?

A poor man owed a large debt to a money-lender, who, desiring the man's beautiful daughter, proposed a deal: he would put a black pebble and a white pebble into an empty money-bag and the girl would have to choose one of them. If she chose the black, she would become his wife and her father's debt would be cancelled; if she chose the white, she could remain with her father. In sheer desperation, the father and daughter agreed. As the money-lender selected the fate-deciding pebbles, from the pebble-strewn path, the girl noticed with horror that he had dishonestly chosen two black ones. He then asked her to reach into the money-bag and select the pebble that was to decide their future. What should she do next?

A tramp, unable to afford cigarettes, collects butt ends. But he was once a man of substance, and therefore refuses to smoke the ends. Instead, he shreds them until he has enough tobacco to make a real cigarette. When he has collected seven ends he has enough tobacco to make one whole cigarette. One lucky day he finds four cigarette ends in the gutter, and then an additional eight in the ashtray of a parked car, three in an old paint tin and five in the lobby of a hotel. He has enough money for a drink and manages to collect fifteen more cigarette ends in the pub. He discovers four in the social security office, six more on his way home, and four in the pocket of an old coat when he gets there. How many whole cigarettes was he able to smoke that day?

Which one of these dice is
different from the other two?

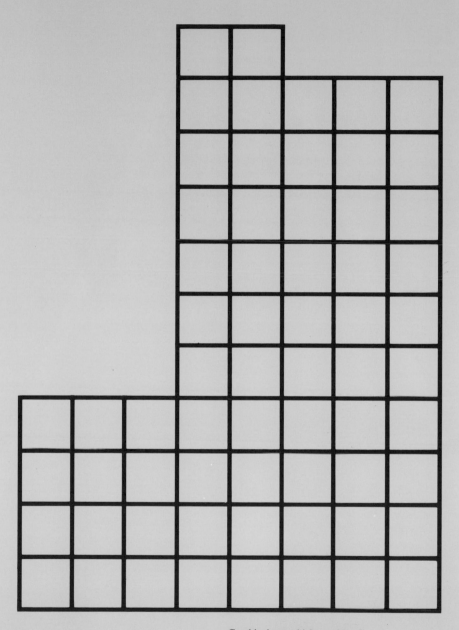

Cut this shape which consists of
sixty-four small squares, into
just two parts. Without turning
either piece over, fit them
together to form an eight by
eight square.

The top rung of the ladder measures ten units, the bottom one sixty units and the rungs are equally spaced. Without measuring, how long is the middle rung?

```
          A
         B B
        R R R
       A A A A
      C C C C C
     A A A A A A
    D D D D D D D
   A A A A A A A A
  B B B B B B B B B
 R R R R R R R R R R
A A A A A A A A A A A
```

Beginning with letter A at the top of the triangle and reading down, always passing from a letter to an adjoining letter, how many ways is it possible to read abracadabra?

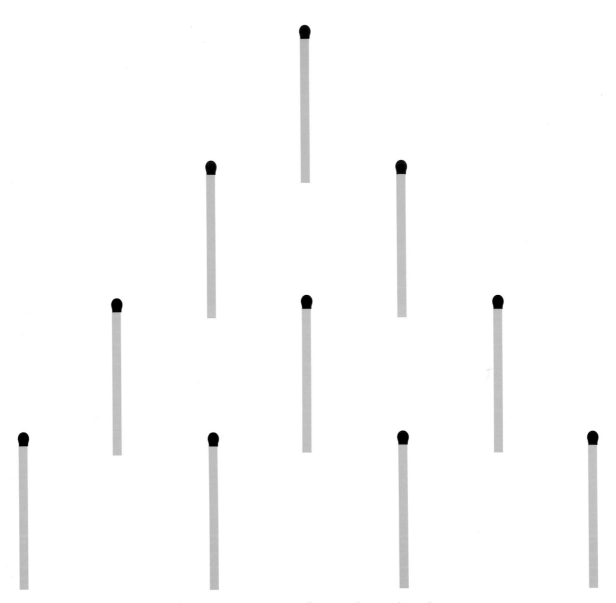

Rearrange three matches so that
the triangular pattern points
down instead of up.

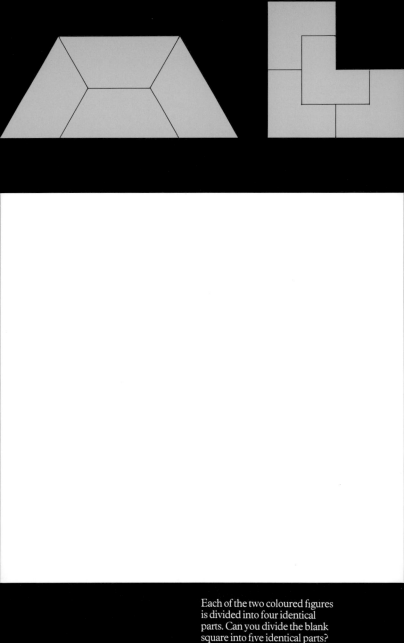

Each of the two coloured figures
is divided into four identical
parts. Can you divide the blank
square into five identical parts?

Everyone knows how to divide
a cake without arguing. One
cuts it, the other chooses which
piece he wants. But can you
suggest a way to let any number
of people divide a cake fairly on
similar lines?

How many slices of pie can be made
by six straight vertical cuts?

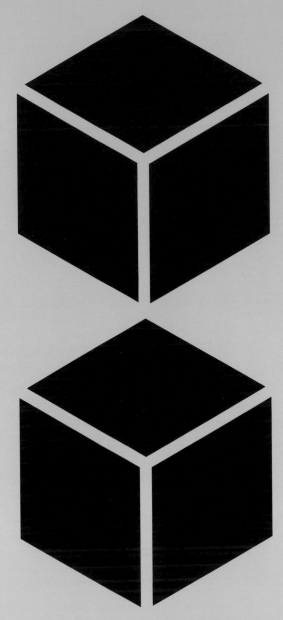

How would you cut a hole in
one cube to enable another
identically-sized cube to pass
through it?

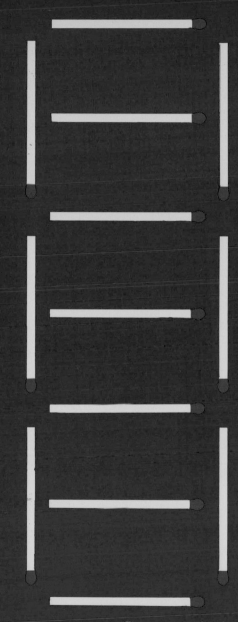

Remove one match and
rearrange the remainder to
make six equal shapes.

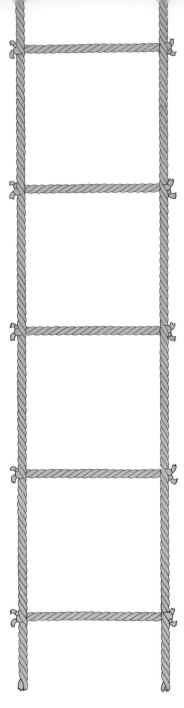

A canal barge is in a lock ten metres long and five metres wide, currently flooded to a depth of two metres. Over the side hangs a rope ladder whose bottom rung is fifteen cm above the surface of the water. The upstream sluice gates open and water pours into the lock at a rate of five hundred litres per second. How soon will the water touch the ladder?

On the first day the beanstalk increased its height by half, on the second day by a third, on the third day by a quarter, and so on.

How long did it take to achieve its maximum height one hundred times its original height?

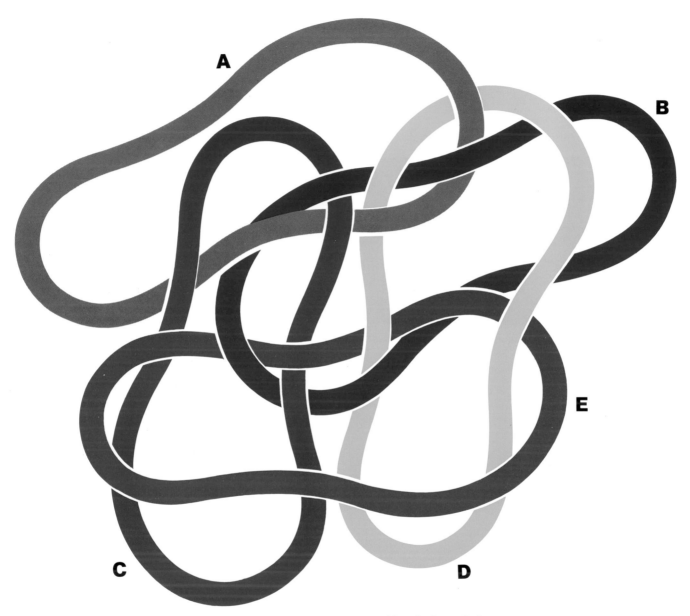

A

B

E

C

D

Which of these five loops of string
must be cut so that the other
loops fall apart?

A

B

C

D

E

F

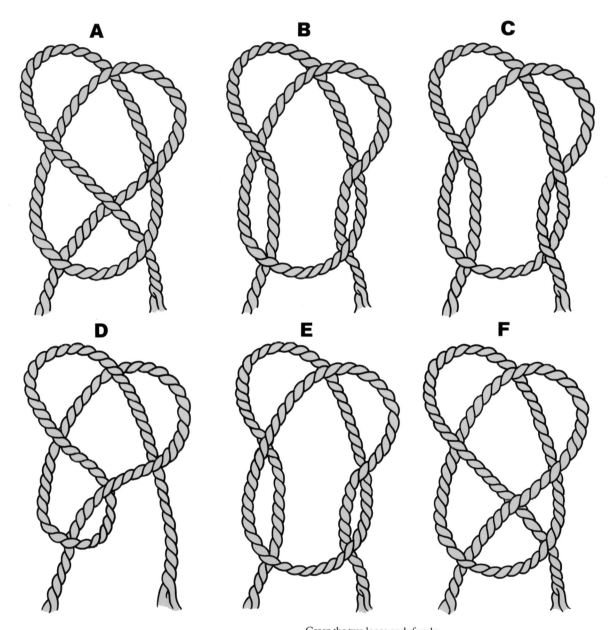

Grasp the two loose ends firmly
in your mind, then imagine
yourself pulling them until you
have a straight piece of rope –
either with a knot or without one.
Which of these six will give you
a knot?

Being very rich, and very eccentric, I own an island on which I live in solitude. Every few days I fly in my seaplane to one of the neighbouring islands to buy provisions. One day I make such a trip to find that it is Sunday and the shops are closed. What is more, I recall that every shop in the entire island group is closed on Sundays. About to give up, I suddenly think of something, and soon I am back on my island complete with food. Whereabouts is my island?

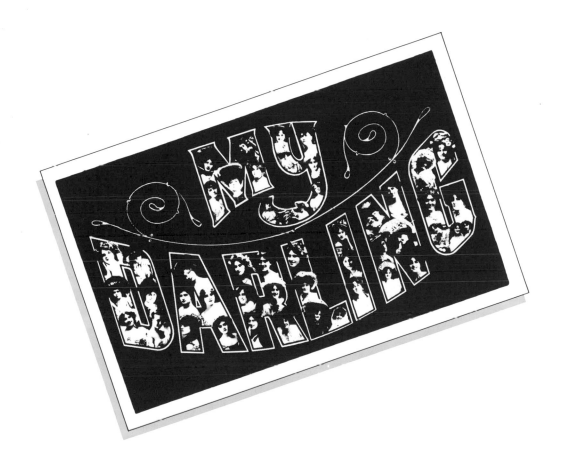

Using only a pair of scissors and no measuring instruments cut the postcard into four pieces, each of which has exactly the same area but a different shape.

Do you see anything curious
about this halfpenny stamp
depicting Columbus, and issued
by the British Colony in the
year 1903?

I bought four cards with matching coloured envelopes to avoid a muddle. But I wish I'd checked before sealing the envelopes. I feel quite sure that: Either the red envelope does not contain a red card, or the yellow envelope does not contain a blue card. Either the green envelope does not contain the yellow card, or the blue envelope does not contain the blue card. Either Matthew should get the green card, or Mark should get the yellow envelope. Either Michael should get the blue envelope, or Martin should get the yellow card. Either the green envelope does not contain the blue card, or Martin should not get the red envelope. How should I address them?

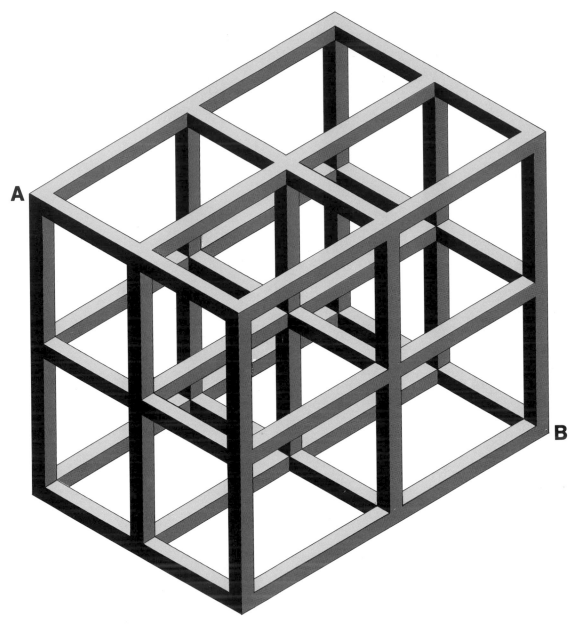

A

B

A building under construction has three rows of vertical steel girders with three girders in a row, and these are connected by horizontal girders on every one of three floors. If you can descend by walking along any horizontal girder and climbing down any vertical one, how many different routes are possible from A to B ? Backward moves are not allowed.

How many rectangular blocks
are there in this construction?
Each measures two by one
by one.

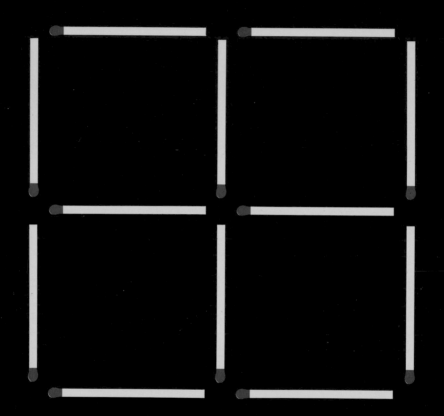

Rearrange two matches to make
seven squares.

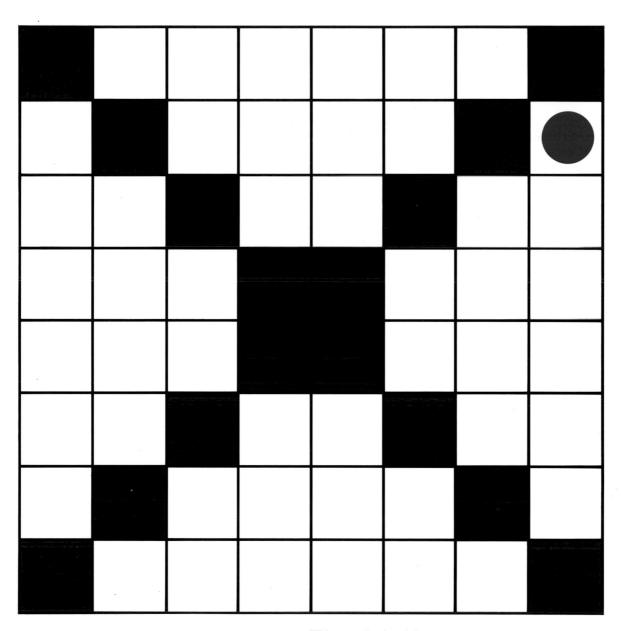

Without moving the existing circle, add seven more to the unshaded squares ensuring that no circle is in line with another, either horizontally, vertically or diagonally.

Without taking your pencil off
the paper, or folding the paper,
cross all the dots with four
straight lines.

What is the minimum number
of colours required to fill in
this outline sketch, given that no
two adjacent areas have the
same colour?

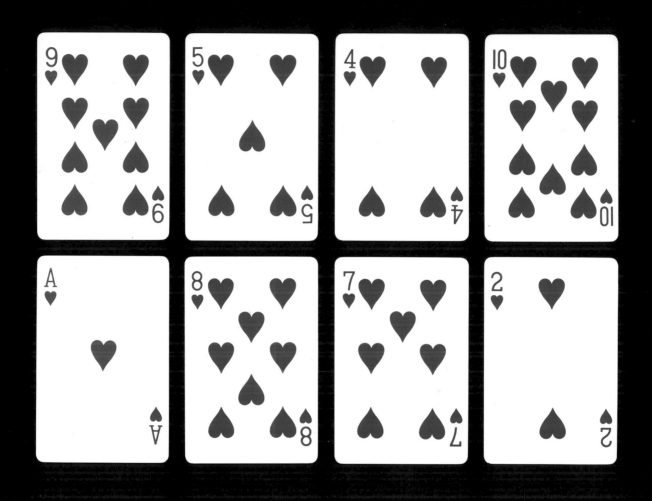

If you turn just two adjacent
cards 180 degrees, the number
of right-side-up hearts on all
eight cards will be the same as
the number of upside-down
hearts. Which two cards should
be turned?

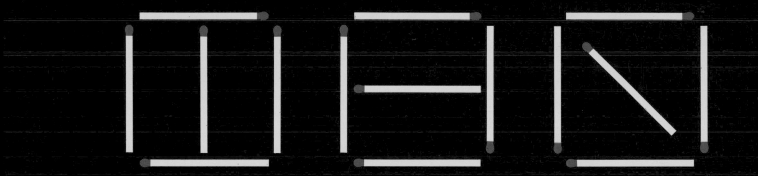

Remove six matches to make ten.

A pilot is setting off for a specific destination, and offers a stranded traveller a lift, insisting that wherever her destination, it can be no more than a few miles out of his way. Given that they are both flying from Buenos Aires, what is his destination?

A river has two bridges spanning it that are exactly one mile from each other. While practising for a boat race, a competitor went upstream. He rowed at a constant rate, and, in doing so, passed under the two bridges. Just underneath the second bridge his cap fell into the water. A further ten minutes passed before he realised that he had lost it. He then turned round and began rowing, still at the same constant rate, in the direction from which he had come. He finally caught up with the cap under the first bridge. How fast does the river flow?

A solid cube is exactly balanced on one of its corners. If you were to slice clean across this cube with a cut parallel to the floor, what shape would the cut surface have?

Rearrange four matches so as to
make six triangles.

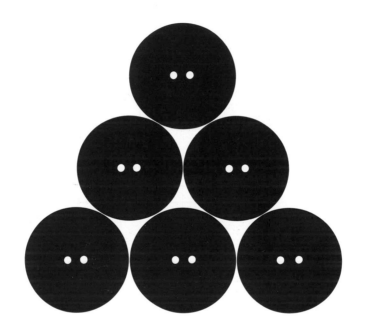

In three moves only, rearrange the pyramid of six buttons to make a circle. A move consists of sliding a button, keeping it flat on the surface, to any new position so long as it comes to rest touching another button. While moving one button, no other button may be jostled or moved.

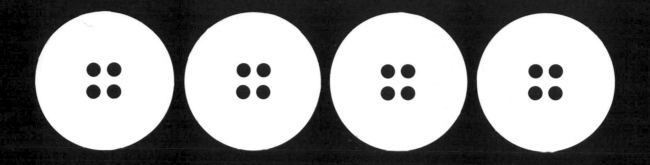

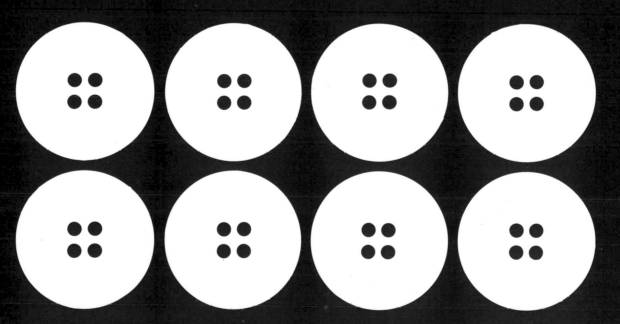

In this game two players take turns to draw buttons, the winner being the person to make the final draw. On each turn a player must claim either a) any number from one pile, or b) an equal number from both. If a game has reached this stage, and it were your turn to claim, how many buttons should you claim to make absolutely certain of winning?

In a Stroke play golf tournament,
there are sixty-eight entrants.
How many matches will there
be in the tournament?

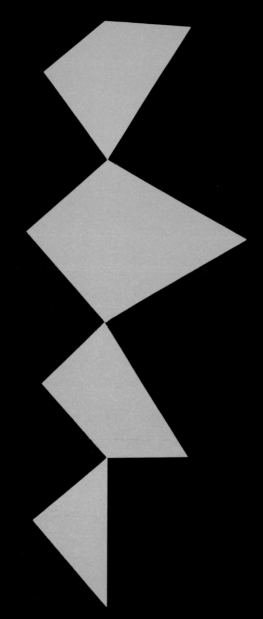

These four pieces are hinged so
they can be folded up into a
regular shape. Is it a triangle or
a square?

Place the numbers one to nine,
one on each vertex and two
along each side, so that each
side adds up to seventeen.

How many equilateral triangles
are there in this diagram? What
are the fewest number of sharp
turns needed if this pattern were
drawn in a continuous line?

Arrange three coins in such a
way that, by turning two over at
a time, you can make them all
appear heads up in exactly
three moves.

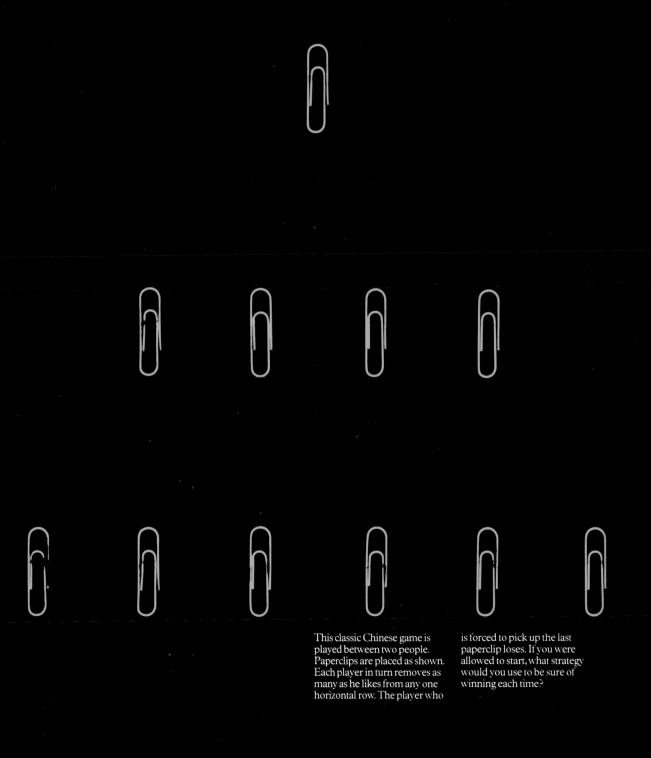

This classic Chinese game is played between two people. Paperclips are placed as shown. Each player in turn removes as many as he likes from any one horizontal row. The player who is forced to pick up the last paperclip loses. If you were allowed to start, what strategy would you use to be sure of winning each time?

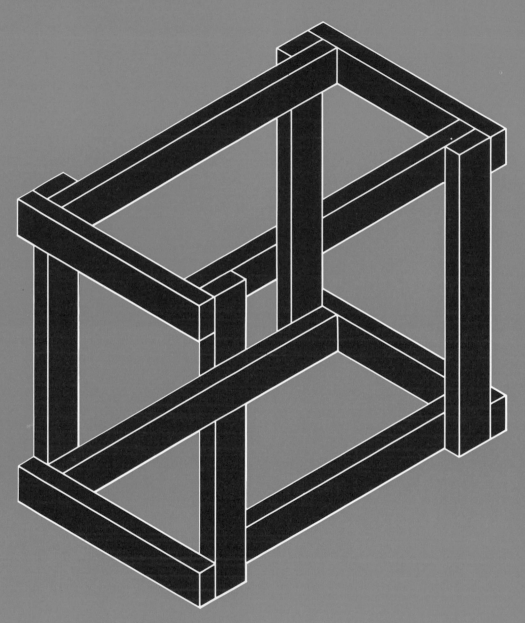

Do you think that by viewing
this object from another angle it
might not be as impossible to
construct as it would appear?

A lateral-thinking engineering consultant tried to persuade his client over an expensive dinner that he could do a crucial job in a fraction of the time his rivals would take. The sceptical client pointed at the checkered tablecloth and said: 'That's like telling me you could cut that cloth into neatly separated red and white squares with a single cut.' Did the engineer get the contract?

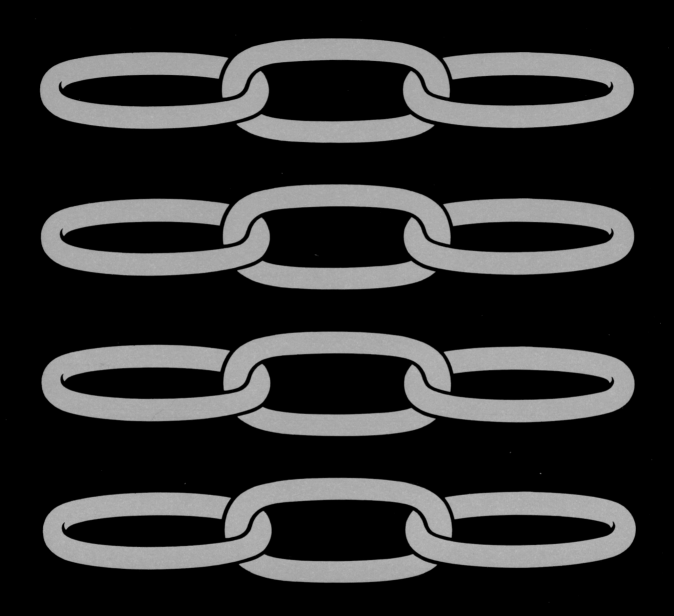

A jeweller was given four segments of silver chain as illustrated and then asked to join them together to make a bracelet. As his charge was ten dollars to cut and reweld a link his bill for forty dollars seemed fair. Would you have been happy to pay this amount?

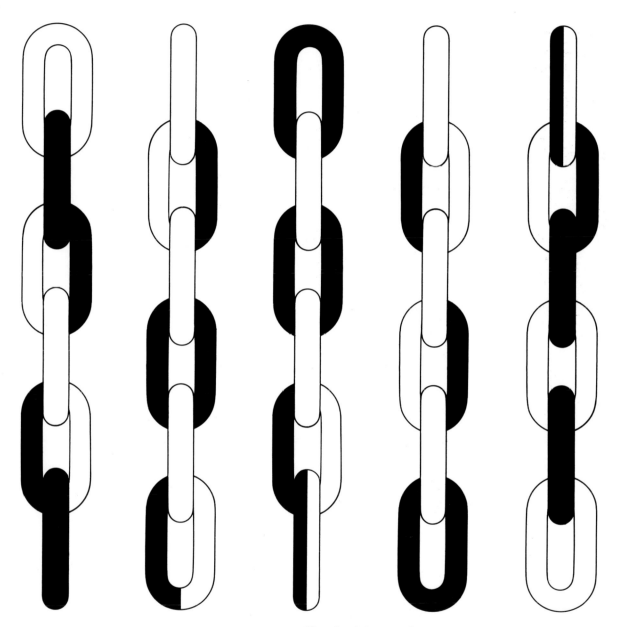

These five chains are made up
of black, white, and half black,
half white links. Which two of
the five chains are identical?

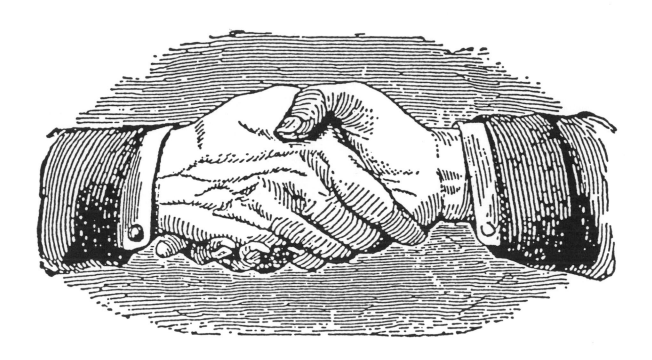

At the introductory meeting of a
political convention, an even
number of delegates shook hands
an odd number of times. What is
a simple way of proving this?

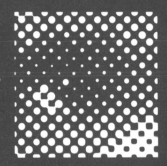

At a secret meeting, everyone
shakes hands exactly once with
every other person present.
Altogether there are forty-five
handshakes. How many people
attended the meeting?

Considering each domino as a fraction, for example the first one in the top row is ³/₄, each row of dominoes adds up to two and a half. Rearrange the fifteen pieces in three rows of five pieces each so that the sum of the fractions in each row is ten.

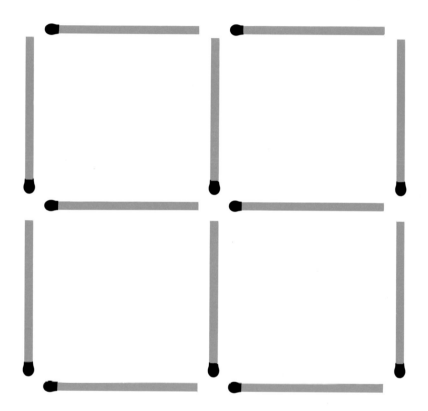

Change the position of four matches to make three small squares all the same size with no matches left over.

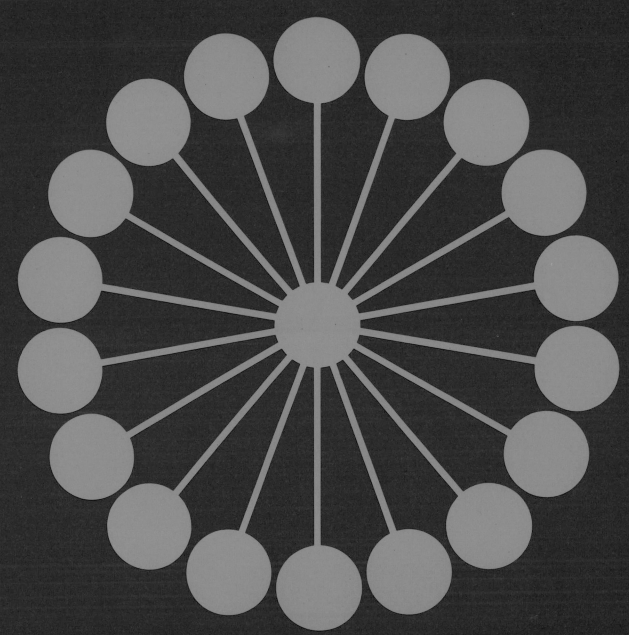

Place the numbers one to nineteen in the circles in such a manner that any three numbers on a straight line total thirty.

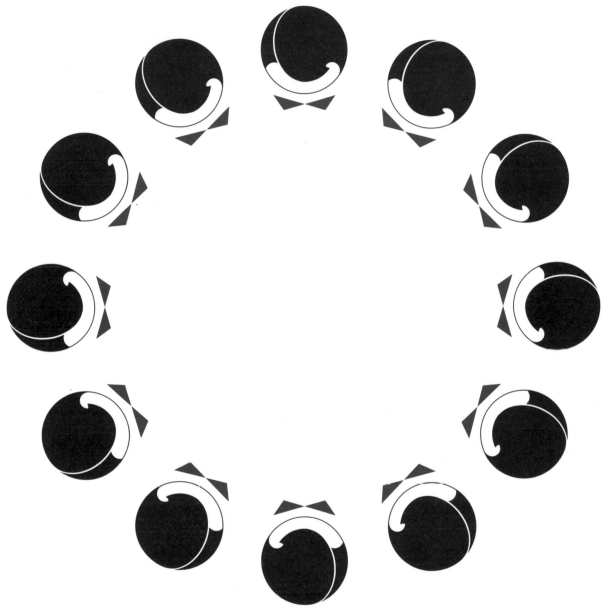

You and a colleague have just taken over a large company and are about to fire the present board. Before entering the boardroom to meet the directors you agree that one of you will become Chairman, the other the Deputy. The decision is left to luck but you agree that whoever ends up firing the last man will become the Deputy. Offering your colleague the opportunity to start, you take turns firing any single person or any two adjacent people. The question is, are you a loser or really the right man to be the new Chairman?

106

Two prisoners are tied together by their hands as shown. Can they separate themselves without cutting the string or untying the knots?

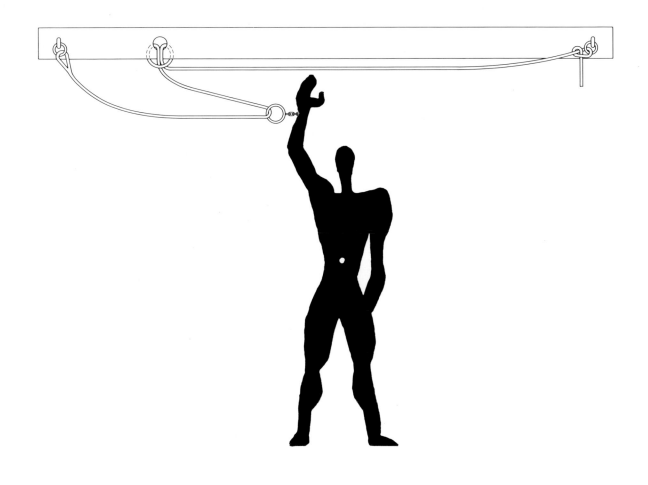

Drawing by Ted Hammond Figure by Le Corbusier

The warder, having secured the prisoner to his satisfaction, ties the loose end of the rope and goes home. The prisoner cannot reach to undo the knot and almost gives up, when he thinks of a solution and escapes still wearing the handcuffs.

After a road accident, four witnesses described the hit and run driver. According to the cabby, he was short and fair-haired, wearing glasses and a blue shirt. The traffic-warden claimed he had dark hair and was of average height, but agreed that he was wearing glasses and a blue shirt. The truck driver thought he was a tall red-head, wearing glasses and a white shirt. The workman said he was small and bald, with a blue shirt but no glasses. It was determined that each witness described only one detail out of four correctly. Every detail was described correctly by at least one witness. What is the correct description of the driver?

Without moving the page, what is the least number of balls which would have to be moved to make the triangle point to the bottom.

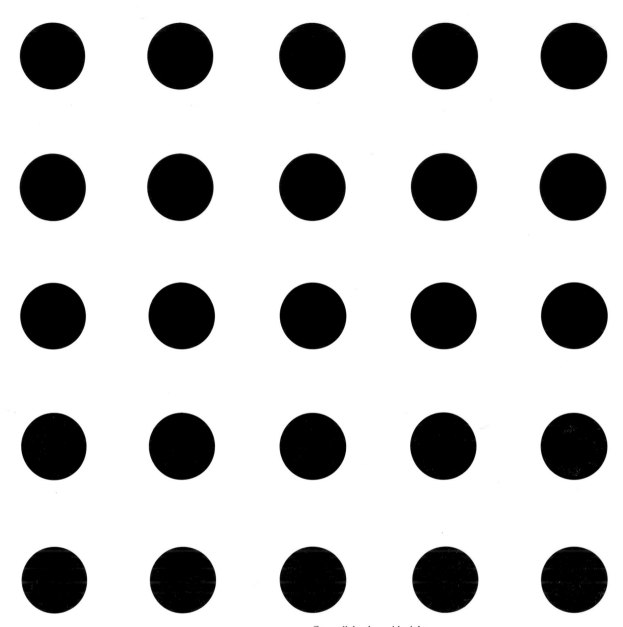

Cross all the dots with eight
straight lines without folding or
taking your pencil off the paper.

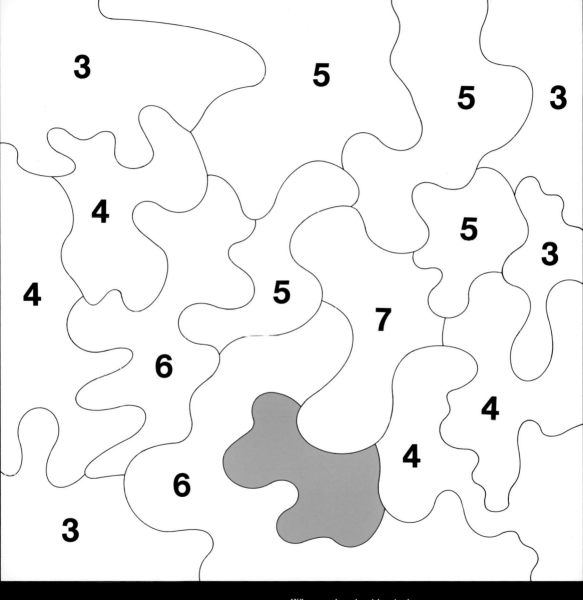

What number should go in the
shaded area?

$$1 + 3 = 4$$

$$1 + 3 + 5 = 9$$

$$1 + 3 + 5 + 7 = 16$$

$$1 + 3 + 5 + 7 + 9 = 25$$

If you add together odd numbers from one upwards you will always get a perfect square. Can you think of a simple visual way to prove that this must always be the case?

T Eliot top bard,

notes putrid tang emanating,

is sad. I'd assign it

a name: gnat

dirt upset on drab pot toilet

What is the most curious aspect
of this verse?

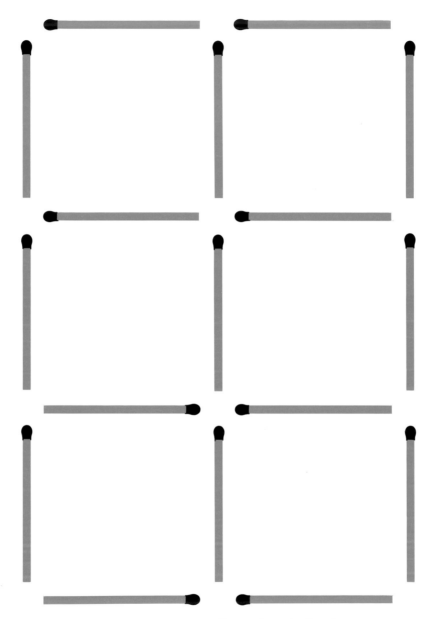

Remove six matches from the six squares so as to leave two perfect squares and no odd matches.

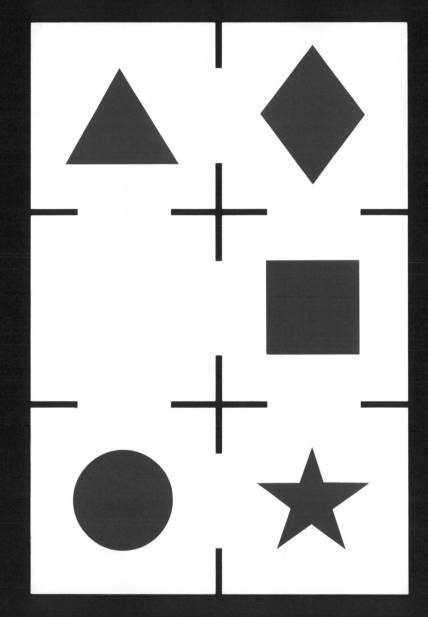

What is the smallest number of moves required to transpose the circle with the star? A move consists of placing one shape at a time onto an adjacent empty square.

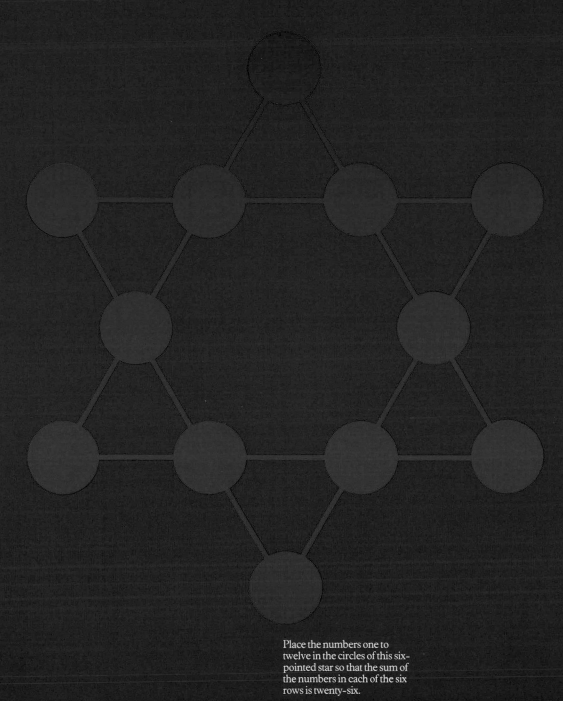

Place the numbers one to
twelve in the circles of this six-
pointed star so that the sum of
the numbers in each of the six
rows is twenty-six.

How many regular hexagons
are there in this figure?

During a country walk, a man and three children encounter a stream. As he is the only one wearing suitable boots, he decides to carry the children over one at a time. Bearing in mind that Ann argues when left alone with either Andrew or Mark, how does he manage to carry them across without an argument breaking out?

To help solve an acute national over-population problem a government issues a radical decree that families should stop having children as soon as they have had one son. After a while, there are some families with only one boy, some with one girl and one boy, some with two girls and one boy, some with three girls and one boy, some with six girls and one boy etc., and some families who only have girls and give up trying for a son. Would boys tend to outnumber girls in this generation? Or vice versa?

Remove three matches from the
five squares so as to leave only
three of the squares.

Supply the missing symbol.

Two farmers were staring into a large barrel partly filled with ale. One of them said brightly: 'Aye it's over half full'. But the other declared, 'Nay 'tis more'n half empty'. How could they prove – without any measuring device – if it was more or less than exactly half full?

Can you tie a knot in the centre
of a handkerchief without
letting go the ends?

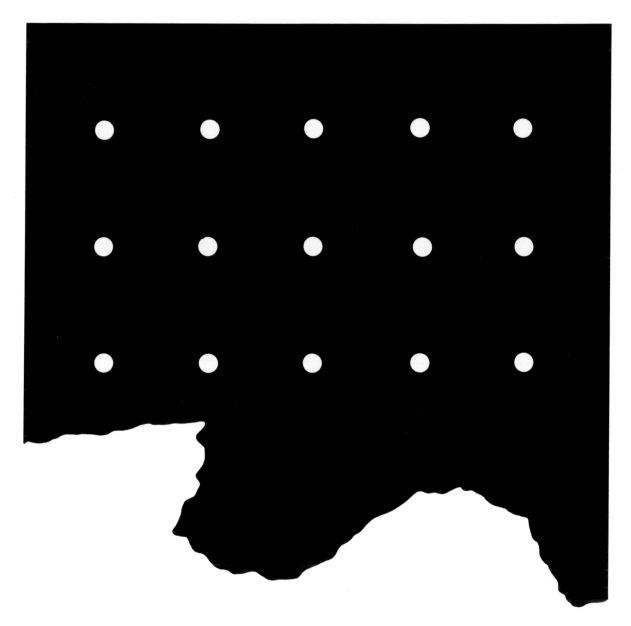

A do-it-yourself enthusiast had an irregular-shaped piece of wood which had a regular pattern of holes. Disliking the holes, and really in search of a piece to make a square table top, he nearly threw it away but was struck with an idea of how to use the board to make a hole-free table top. How did he do it?

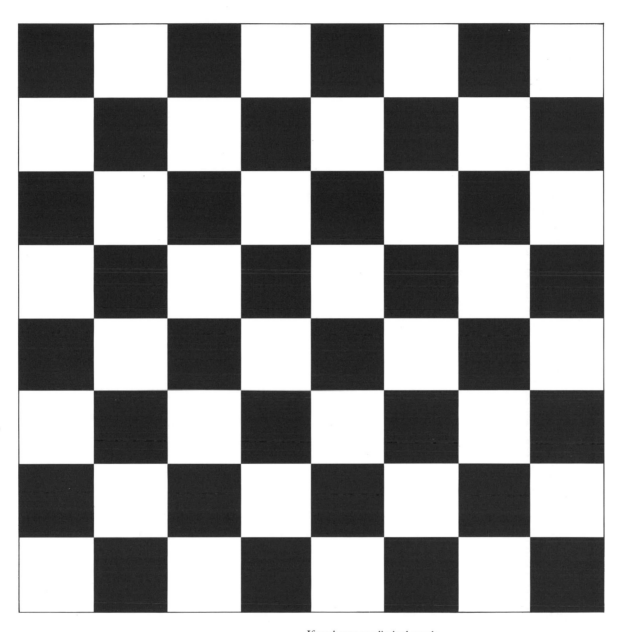

If you have an unlimited supply, placing one on the first square, two on the second square, four on the third and so on, how many counters would be required to cover each square of this board?

Moving two adjacent glasses at
a time without transposing
them, and with only four moves,
change the positions so that
each glass alternately holds red
or white wine.

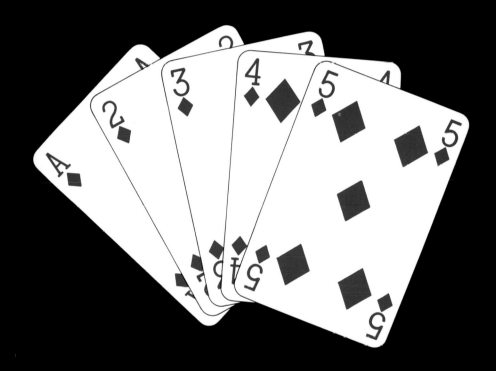

Arrange the cards to form a
regular rectangle divided into
five areas. The ace card should
show in its entirety and the
other four cards must be placed
so the remainder of the area is
equally divided between them.

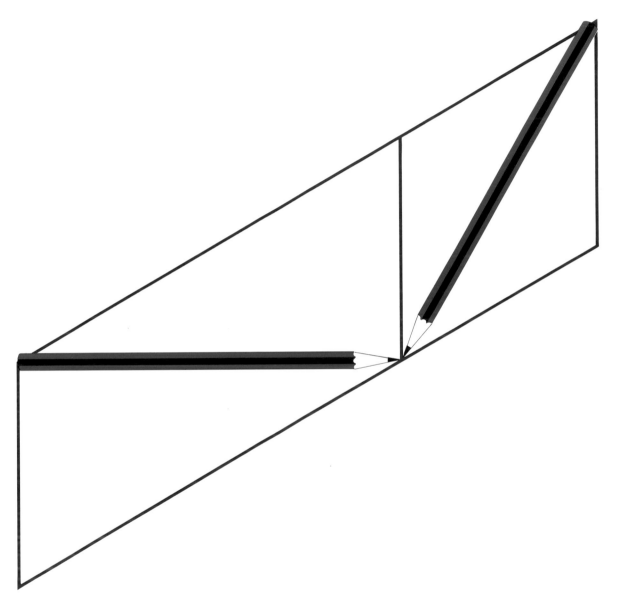

Which one of these pencils is shorter than the other?

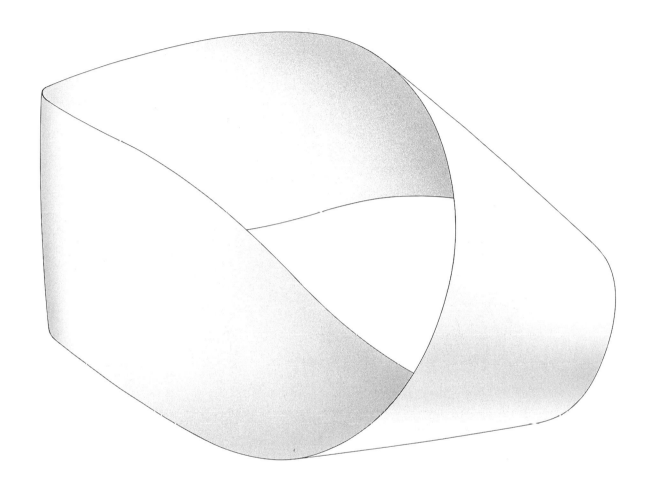

A Moebius band is a curious topological model which has only one surface and one edge. If the band was cut in half along its length, what would be the result?

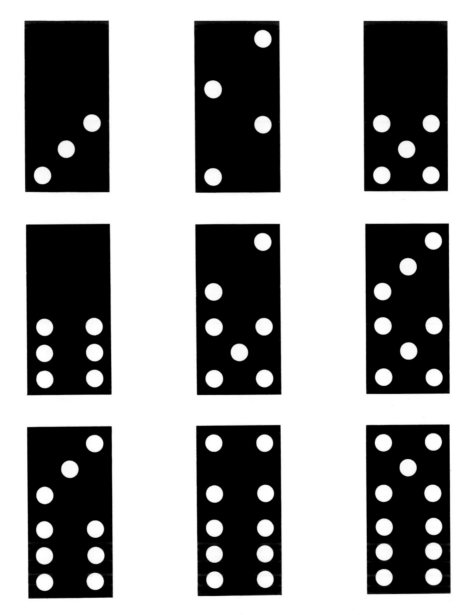

Rearrange the dominoes so that
the sum of the dots on every
vertical, horizontal and diagonal
row totals twenty-one.

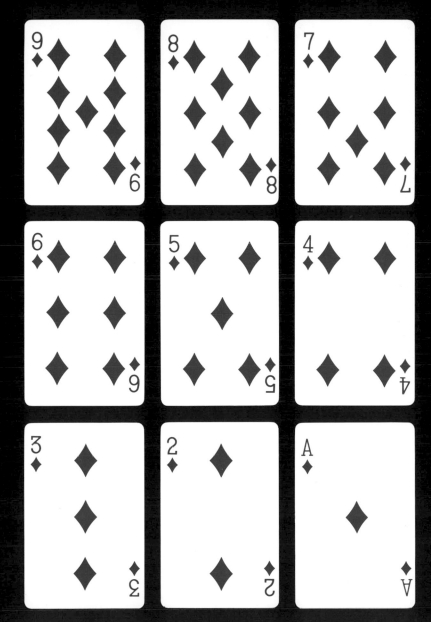

Rearrange the cards in this formation so that each horizontal, vertical and diagonal line of three adds up to fifteen.

Two tramps are sharing a bottle of wine. They want to be sure that each one of them drinks exactly half the available wine but they have no glasses, or any other container, or anything else with which to mark the bottle. Can it be done?

An uneducated
and illiterate
cook fulfilled
his ambition
and opened
a restaurant.
He acquired
twenty-eight
bottles of rare
brandy and employed
a poor relative as a waiter.
Unfortunately the illiterate cook
was unable to count over ten, and
knowing his relative was partial to
good brandy and dishonest into the
bargain, he took the precaution of
arranging his rare brandy in racks so
that each side always totalled nine.
The racks consisted of three rows
of three bins each with room for
up to five bottles. On two separate
occasions the waiter stole four
bottles, but he always rearranged
the remainder so that each side still
made nine and the cook had no idea
he had been cheated. How were the
bottles arranged at each stage?

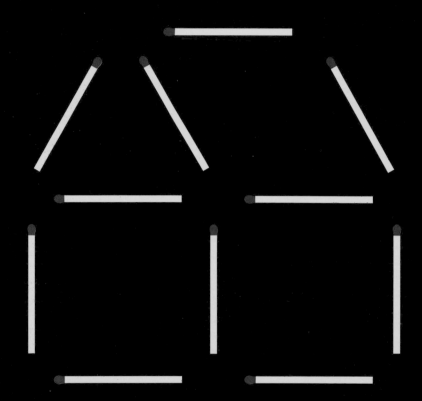

Move one match to make the
house face east instead of west.

In the game of Monopoly, a pair of dice is thrown: the combined score determines how far a player can go. A player is so placed that throwing a five will take him to Bond Street, eight to Park Lane, or ten to Mayfair.

I own all of these properties, but can afford a hotel on just one of them. Where should I place it to maximise the probability that my opponent will land on it on his next throw?

This image represents a piece of
paper which has been cut and
folded. Can you visually
unravel it to form a rectangle?

How can this paper be folded
along the creases shown, so that
the pages are in correct order
when made into an eight-page
leaflet?

Without measuring, what is the
ratio between the full height
and the width of this top hat?

A young enterprising stockbroker interviewed three candidates for position of clerk. Since all three were equally suitable he decided to give them a test of logic. All three were scrupulously honest, so when they were asked to close their eyes while he put a hat on each of their heads, they did not cheat in order to see the hat they were wearing. Ordering them to open their eyes he explained that he may have put on top hats or bowlers, but whoever saw a bowler hat was to raise a hand. All three put up a hand. The winning candidate, the stockbroker explained, would be the first to infer correctly whether he was wearing a bowler or top hat, providing he was able to prove it.

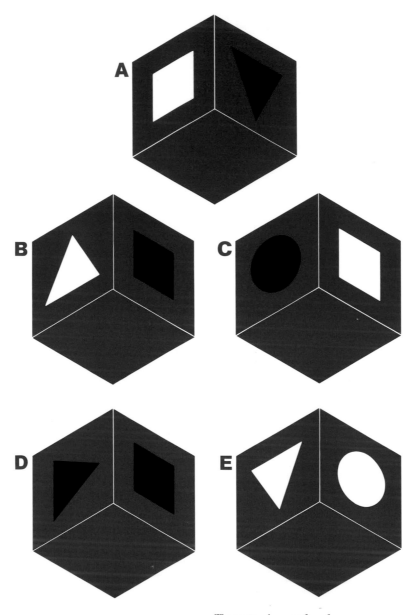

The same cube, seen from five
different angles, has one of six
symbols on each side. What
symbol would you see on the
top side of each of the five cubes if
you could peer over the top edge?

Rearrange these shapes and
turn over one of them to form a
letter of the alphabet.

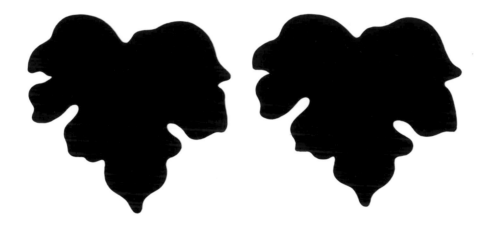

Many people believe in an after life; the Vikings believed in Valhalla and Red Indians in the 'happy hunting grounds'. One rather obscure religious sect in California believed in Genesis. They thought that all people in heaven were the same youthful age, were uninhibited, did not wear clothes, and spent the days laughing, singing and dancing in the Garden of Eden. The elderly founder of this sect duly passed away and arrived in heaven. After a short while he observed Adam and Eve among the throng. In the circumstances, how was he able to distinguish them from the others?

If you add the age of a man to
the age of his wife you get a
combined age of 91 years. He is
now twice as old as she was
when he was as old as she is
now. How old are they?

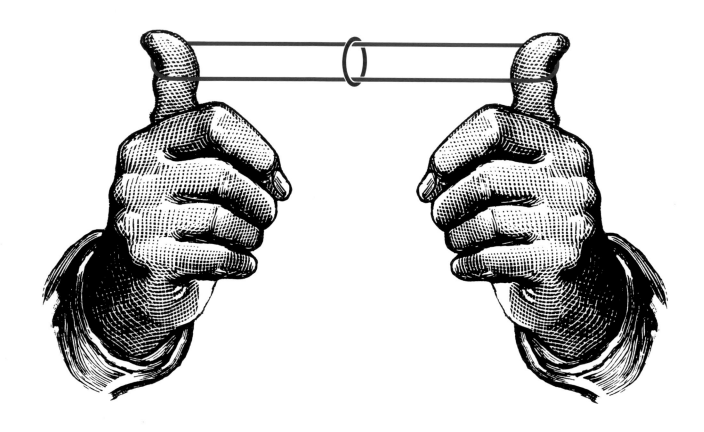

Thread a looped string through
a ring and hold it taut between
two thumbs. How can you
release the ring, using only your
two little fingers while keeping
the string taut?

Laetitia has a large one
And so has Cousin Luce;
Eliza has a little one,
But big enough for use.

Each child has a little one
Enclosed within a clout;
In fact all females have one –
No girls are born without.

Hermaphrodites have none;
Mermaids are minus too;
Nell Gwyn possessed a double share,
If all we read be true.

Lasciviousness there has its source;
Harlots its use apply
Without it lust has never been
And even love would die.

'Tis known to all in nuptial bliss
In carnal pleasure found.
Without it love becomes extinct –
The word is but a sound.

Now tell me what my object is,
But pause before you guess it;
If you be mother, mate or man,
I swear you don't possess it.

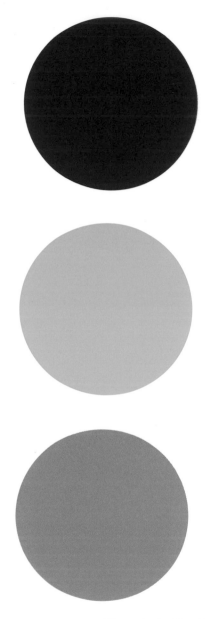

All motorists familiar with traffic lights know the four signals that are used by taking red, red and yellow, yellow and green. But how many signals could be represented if all possible combinations were allowed, assuming that at least one colour shows?

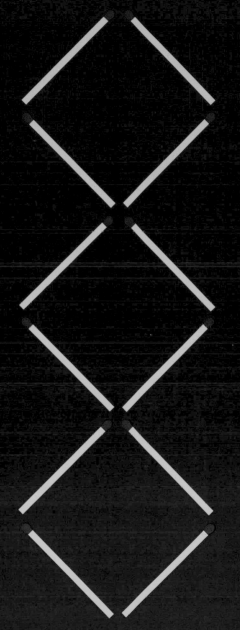

Rearrange these twelve matches
to form seven diamonds.

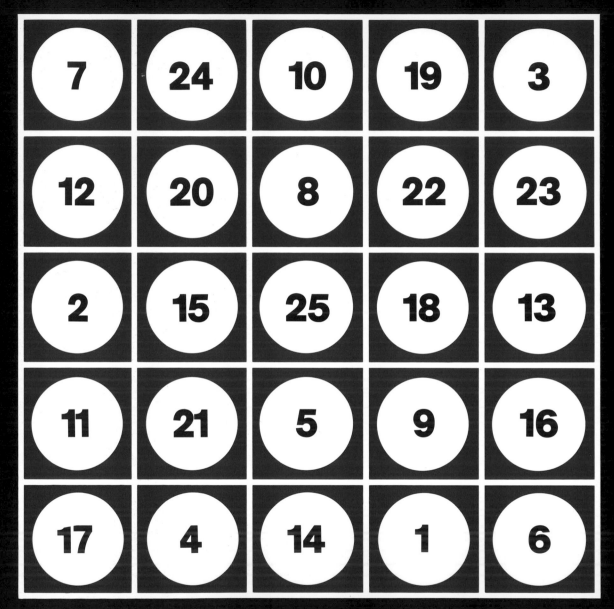

By exchanging one number with another, rearrange the chart so that it reads in numerical order; one to five across the top row, six to ten across the second, etcetera. What is the minimum number of moves required to do this, and what basic method can best be applied?

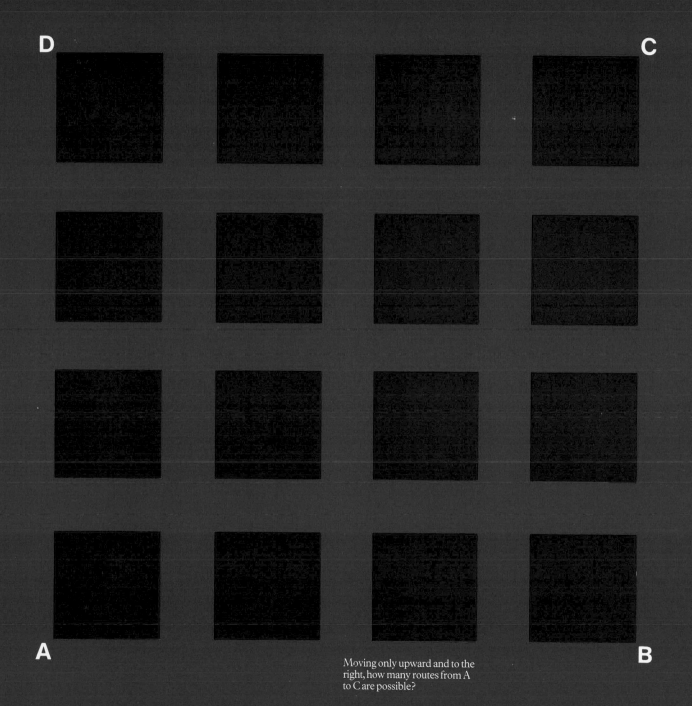

D   C

A   B

Moving only upward and to the
right, how many routes from A
to C are possible?

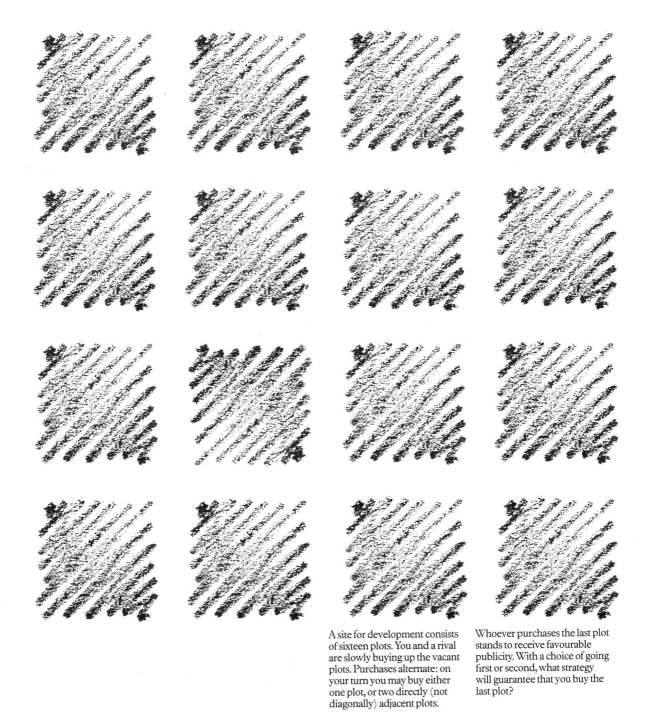

A site for development consists of sixteen plots. You and a rival are slowly buying up the vacant plots. Purchases alternate: on your turn you may buy either one plot, or two directly (not diagonally) adjacent plots.

Whoever purchases the last plot stands to receive favourable publicity. With a choice of going first or second, what strategy will guarantee that you buy the last plot?

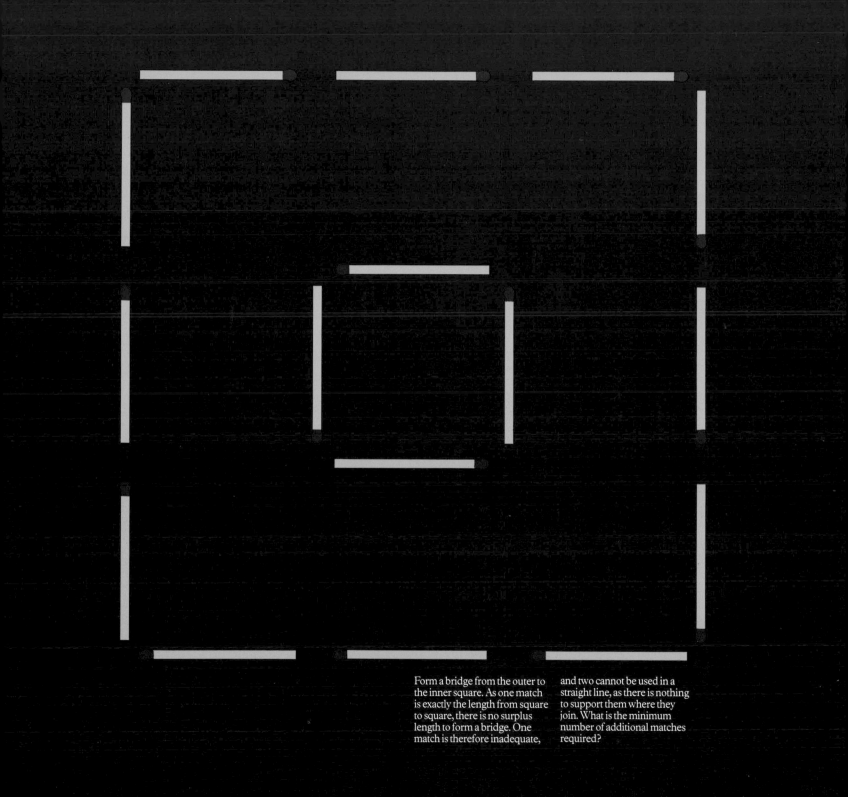

Form a bridge from the outer to the inner square. As one match is exactly the length from square to square, there is no surplus length to form a bridge. One match is therefore inadequate, and two cannot be used in a straight line, as there is nothing to support them where they join. What is the minimum number of additional matches required?

At an athletics meeting there are twenty-one entrants for each of the three events: 100 metres, 200 metres and 400 metres. There are fewer than sixty-three competitors because some are taking part in two races and some in all three. In fact, there are at least three people doing every possible combination of one, two or three races, and each such group contains a different number. Given that the largest group is those who are running 400 metres but not participating in any other race, how many are running 100 metres and 200 metres but not 400 metres?

Two men have an argument about the merits of their two favourite horses. To settle the disagreement, they decide to stage a race, the wager being an oil well. Since neither wishes to lose in public they hit on the idea of a slow horse race: the last horse to pass the post will be announced the winner. On the appointed day the race begins. As it progresses the horses decrease their speed until practically at a standstill. Frustrated, the jockeys dismount and after a lengthy consultation leap back on the horses and finish the race by dashing to the post. Assuming the conditions of the race are observed and that neither jockey betrays his employer, what do you think they decided to do?

If a rubber ball is dropped from the Leaning Tower of Pisa at a height of ninety metres from the ground, and on each rebound the ball rises exactly one-tenth of its previous height, what distance will it travel before it comes to rest?

4

16

8

64

32

1024

Complete this sequence.

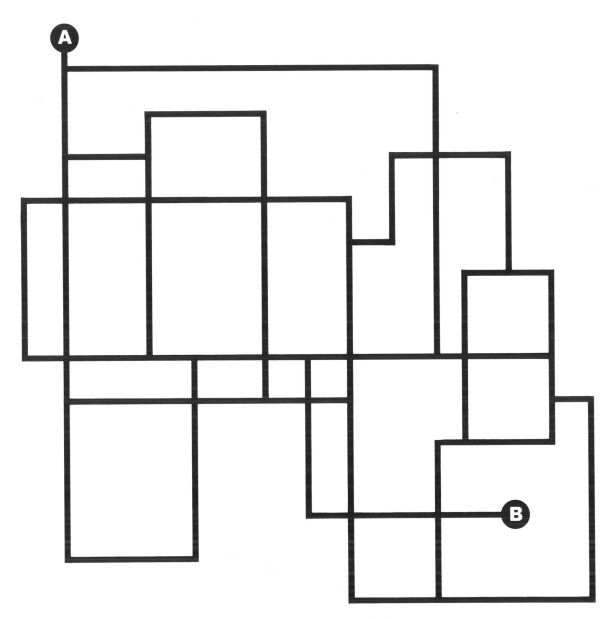

You are at A and wish to direct someone to B. What is the simplest set of instructions you could give?

A traveller comes to a fork in the road and does not know which path to take to reach his destination. There are two men at the fork, one of whom always lies while the other always tells the truth. He doesn't know which is which. He may ask one of the men only one question to find his way. What is his question and which man does he ask?

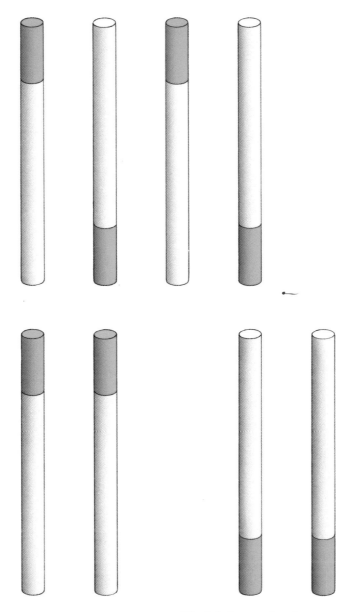

What is the least number of moves required to rearrange the first row of cigarettes into the second? A move consists of sliding a cigarette to an empty position or leap-frogging one cigarette over another.

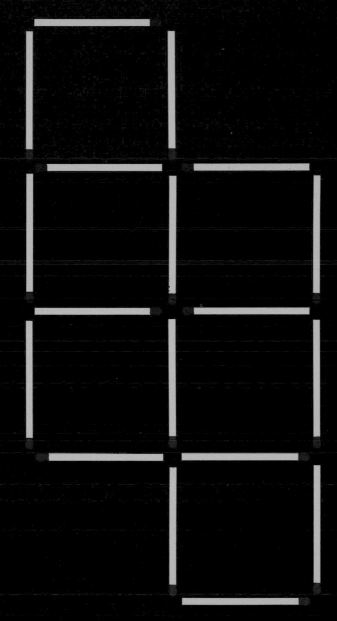

Rearrange two matches to make four equal squares, with every match forming the side of a square.

This pattern starts from the top and works downwards. Each row is worked out from the line above using the same rule.

What is it? If you add more rows to the base, how will the dots be coloured. Will the pattern ever repeat?

Moving one counter only, make
two rows of four.

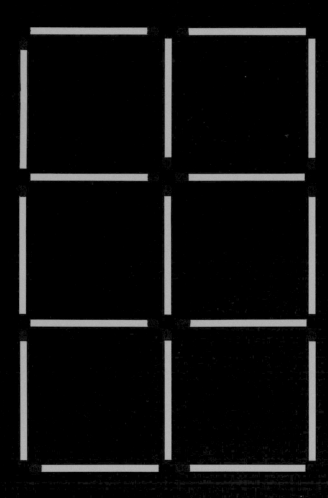

Rearrange two matches to make
six squares.

Every day
The PLAT du JOUR
is BOOKS...

A lawyer had ten volumes of legal reference which he rarely consulted. One day he discovered a bookworm had eaten its way in a straight line from the front cover of volume 1 to the back cover of volume 10. Each book was two inches thick. How far did the bookworm travel?

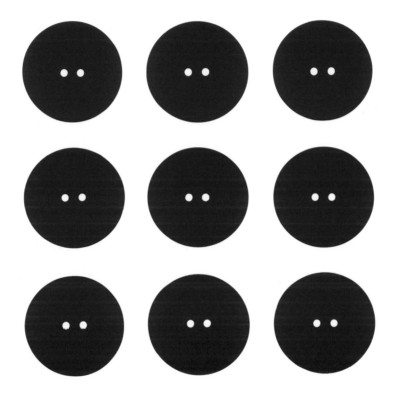

Arrange the nine buttons in
such a manner that they form
ten rows, with three buttons in
each row.

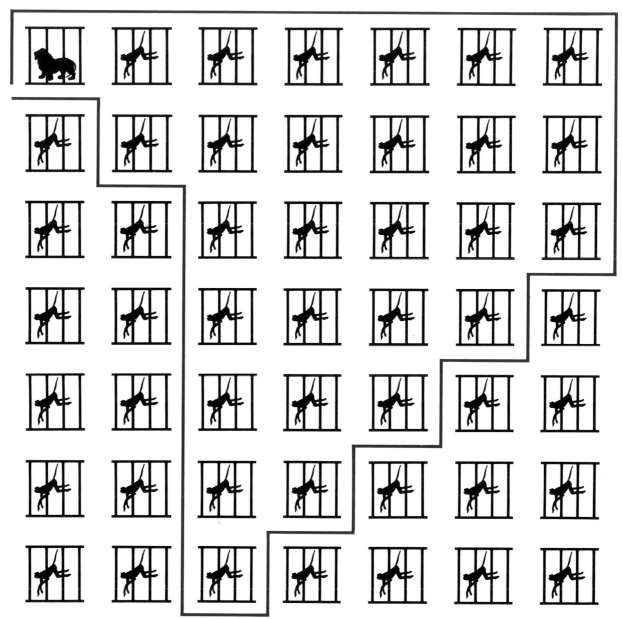

A zookeeper visits forty-nine cages, beginning and ending at the lion's cage. His orders are to pass an uneven number of cages along any row before he makes a turn, and he cannot walk twice along any portion of his route. The red line, which takes him past twenty-eight cages, shows his present route. Find a route that, complying with the orders, will take him past the greatest possible number of cages. The path must begin and end at the lion's cage.

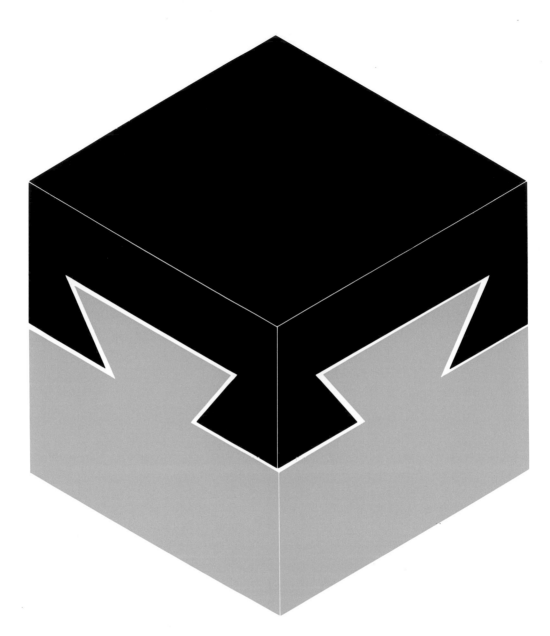

How would you separate these
two blocks, which are held
together by a dovetail joint?

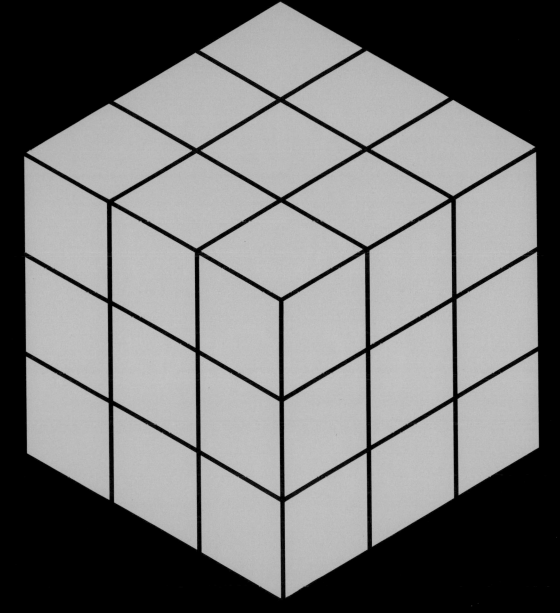

After Xerxes was defeated by the Greeks, he went back to the oracle at Delphi, taking as payment a cube of gold. He asked the oracle what his chances would be if he were to try to defeat them once again.

Now the oracle suspected (correctly) that the cube was in fact lead plated with gold, so she told him: 'Cut the cube into twenty-seven smaller ones. Place them in a leather bag, and draw one cube at random. Roll it like a die. If it comes to rest gold face uppermost, your next campaign will succeed.' What were Xerxes' chances of getting a gold face?

SWIMS

MOW

NOON

WIM

What do these apparently unrelated
words have in common?

I met a widow, who lived with her step-daughter.
I married her. My father fell in love with the
step-daughter of my wife, and married her.
My wife became the mother-in-law of my
own father; my wife's step-daughter is my
step-mother, and I am the step-father of my
step-mother. My step-mother, who is the
step-daughter of my wife, has a boy; he
is my step-brother, because he is the son of
my father and of my step-mother; but as
he is the son of my wife's step-daughter, so is
my wife the grandmother of the boy, and
I am the grandfather of my step-brother.
My wife also has a boy, my step-mother is
consequently his step-sister and is also his
grandmother, because he is the child of her
step-son; and my father is the brother-in-law
of my son. My son is the grandson of my
father. Who is my grandfather?

Arrange five coins so that every
coin touches every other coin.

Taking up one black counter at a time, pass it over two white counters and place it on a third; in six moves only, repeat this operation until there is one black counter on each of the six white counters. Moves may be made in either direction round the circle and black counters may jump over individual white counters, or one black on top of a white counter.

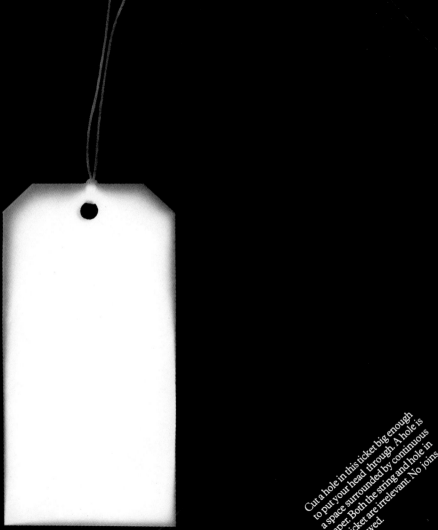

Cut a hole in this ticket big enough
to put your head through. A hole is
a space surrounded by continuous
paper. Both the string and hole in
ticket are irrelevant. No joins
allowed.

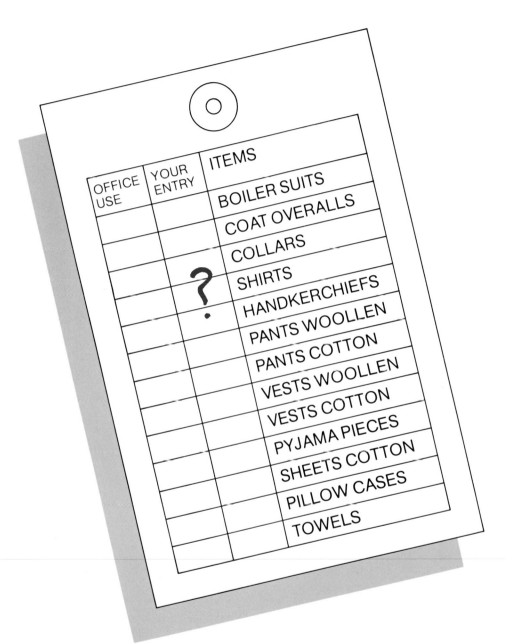

OFFICE USE	YOUR ENTRY	ITEMS
		BOILER SUITS
		COAT OVERALLS
		COLLARS
	?	SHIRTS
		HANDKERCHIEFS
		PANTS WOOLLEN
		PANTS COTTON
		VESTS WOOLLEN
		VESTS COTTON
		PYJAMA PIECES
		SHEETS COTTON
		PILLOW CASES
		TOWELS

A man wears a clean shirt every day. If he drops off his laundry and picks up the previous week's load every Monday night, how many shirts must he own to keep him going?

174

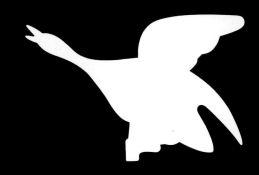

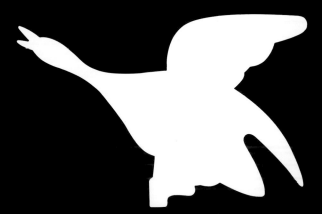

The driver of a truckload of ducks is flagged down by the police for a weight check. As he drives onto the weighbridge, he notices that he is just over his permitted ten tons. Then he has an idea. He bangs on the cab with a spanner. Alarmed, many of the ducks take to the air and flap about. Will the weight on the weighbridge be reduced?

Three rats descending the mooring rope after a long sea voyage meet up with three rats ascending the same rope. One rat can jump over another, but will fall if he tries to either jump over more than one rat at a time, or walk backwards along the rope. Is it possible for the trios to exchange places without any rat falling or leaving the rope?

A dealer bought a painting for $70, sold it for $80, bought it back for $90, and sold it again for $100. How much profit did he make?

'If the puzzle you solved
before you solved
the puzzle you solved
after you solved
the puzzle you solved
before you solved
this one, was harder than
the puzzle you solved
after you solved
the puzzle you solved
before you solved
this one, was
the puzzle you solved
before you solved
this one harder than
this one?'

Solutions

1

Only four. One which is yellow on the front side. One which is yellow with one blue leaf. One which is yellow with two adjacent blue leaves. One which is yellow with two non-adjacent blue leaves. All other patterns possible appear on the reverse side of one of these four.

2

Starting on any point, the answer lies in placing the second and each successive coin on points which enable you to slide them to the starting point vacated by the previous coin.

3

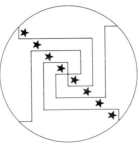

4

Two hundred and four squares.

5

Cut just one link.

6

To simplify the problem, visually reduce the circle to a square, divide the area as illustrated into four, and then add to each portion the remaining segments of the circle. The result is four exactly equal pieces each of which contains two stars.

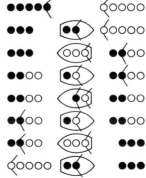

7

If you try to work out the length of each successive trip, you are making life very difficult for yourself. At a combined speed of six miles an hour, the two take ten minutes to meet. At a constant speed of nine miles an hour, the dog, will cover just a mile and a half.

8

Fifteen bees.

9

The 8 blocks have 48 faces altogether. Three pairs of faces are mated.
48 – 6 = 42

10

TOP FLOOR						GROUND FLOOR					
1	5	1	3	1	4	1	2	1	1	1	1
5		5	2		1	2		2	1		1
1	5	1	3	1	3	1	2	1	1	2	1

Before: After: Before: After:
24 men 18 men 12 men 9 men

If you look at the diagrams, you will see that the 'before' boxes total 36 men, and the 'after' boxes total 27 men. A difference of 9 prisoners.

11

12

Six arrows will score 100 by registering 17, 17, 17, 17, 16, 16.

13

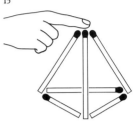

14

The most simple way of tackling this problem is to imagine that the 7 pets are fed 4 biscuits each. This accounts for 28 biscuits, leaving 4 biscuits over. These can be distributed, one each, to four dogs. So there must be 3 cats since 4 dogs and three cats makes 7 pets.

15

16

Since opposite sides of a dice always add up to seven, and the first and third dice have the same vertical orientation, the numbers must be a one and a six. In fact, modern dice are always marked counter-clockwise in serial order, so the top face would be a one and the bottom a six.

17

E(ight) N(ine)

18

4 shoes, 3 socks. Of 4 shoes, 2 must be of the same brand; of 3 socks, 2 must be the same colour.

19

Eight grapes.

20

This problem upsets a lot of people. They argue that since a spoonful of pure vinegar is exchanged for a spoonful which is not pure oil, there must be more vinegar in the oil which must therefore be more contaminated. In fact, they must be equally contaminated no matter how much oil or vinegar is actually transferred or how much mixing takes place. The vinegar which comes back in the second spoonful has done a round trip. So we subtract this amount of vinegar from the original spoonful. What is left in both spoonfuls is equal, so an equal amount of oil and vinegar are exchanged. Another way to look at it is to note that the total volume in each glass is unchanged by the operation; the net volume transferred from A to B exactly cancels that which went from B to A.

21

2592 feet. Since the building contains 10 odd nodes a complete tour will require 5 separate journeys. This means that 4 back-trackings will have to be made. Clearly, as many of these 4 as possible should be the short inner corridors, but experiment shows that at least 2 back-trackings must be made along outer corridors. The total tour will therefore be 10 inner walks plus 2 inner back-trackings of 100 feet each, plus 10 outer walks plus 2 outer back-trackings of 116 feet each. Total 2592. Such a tour could be commenced from any of the eight outside corners, an example being: CBABFAEFEDACDGLGHLJ HJKLDK.

22

99. This number holds true regardless of the manner in which the puzzle is assembled. The proof is simple. We start with 100 pieces and end up with a single cluster. Each move reduces the number of clusters by one. Hence 99 moves.

23

If only one mole is present, he must be Bertie. But if there are two, they must be Albert and Cedric!

24

Thirty-two days.

25

Y	B	W	G
G	R	Y	B
B	W	G	R
R	Y	B	W

26

Reading horizontally from left to right, line by line, there is a series of one symbol, then one two, then one two three, and so on. Once the nth symbol in a series is established it does not change. The missing symbol, being fourth in such a series, is:

27

The impulsive answer is that the bottle is worth £1 and the beer £2 more; but that makes £1 + £3, which is £4 in all. The correct answer is the beer is worth £2.50, the bottle 50p.

28

Although Klaus's arrival is random, the tram timetable is run with German precision. Trams run every twelve minutes in each direction with the southbound arriving two minutes after the northbound one. Whenever you arrive at the stop, the odds are five to one in favour of getting a northbound tram.

29

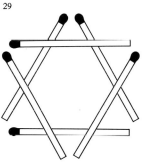

30

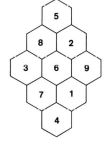

31

Gordon is taller than the defender, so he is not the defender or the goalkeeper. He is the striker. The goalkeeper is not Gordon and not Stanley (a married man). He is Bobby. By elimination, Stanley is the defender.

32

Yes. Suppose the three friends have cycled thirty times with these results: For the first ten days the order of finish is Matthew, Mark, Luke. For the next ten days it is Mark, Luke, Matthew. For the last ten days it is Luke, Matthew, Mark. Matthew arrived before Mark twenty days out of thirty. Mark arrived before Luke twenty days out of thirty. Luke arrived before Matthew twenty days out of thirty.

33

30		44		43		33
	49		54		47	
41		35		36		38
	48		50		52	
37		39		40		34
	53		46		51	
42		32		31		45

34

Each number is the sum of the three numbers; above, above left and left. The missing number is 63.

35

```
  5478
+1624
+9638
─────
 16740
```

36

Each cube must bear a 0, 1 and 2. This leaves only six faces for the remaining seven digits, but the same face can be used for 6 and 9, depending on how the cube is turned. The puzzle shows 3, 4, 5 on the right cube, and therefore its hidden faces must be 0, 1 and 2. On the left cube one can see 1 and 2 and so its hidden faces must be 0, 6 (= 9), 7 and 8.

37

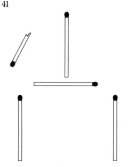

If you take a sheet of paper and mark it as in the drawing, you will find that when you roll it into cylindrical form, with the line outside, it will appear as a column. It will be seen that the spiral (in one complete turn) is merely the hypotenuse of a right-angled triangle, of which the length and width of the paper are the other two sides. In the puzzle the lengths of the two sides of the triangle are 12 metres (one-fifth of 60 metres) and 9 metres. Therefore the hypotenuse is 15 metres. The length of the garland is therefore five times as long: 75 metres.

38

Four colours are sufficient.

39

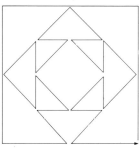

40

The 38 items are: Bag, Basket, Bicycle, Book, Boot, Bucket, Chair, Comb, Cup, Dice, Drum, Eye-bath, Grinder, Hammer, Hat, Hot-water-bottle, Iron, Jug, Kettle, Ladle, Locomotive, Mill, Mirror, Mug, Penknife, Pencil-sharpener, Pipe, Purse, Racquet, Revolver, Ring, Scales, Spoon, Tap, Toast-rack, Trumpet, Typewriter, Watch.

41

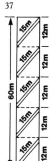

42

Possible combinations are: All faces black = 1. One white face = 1. Two white faces = 2 (adjacent or opposite). Three white faces = 2 (with or without a common corner). Four white faces = 2 (blacks adjacent or opposite). Five white faces = 1. There are nine distinguishable ways to colour the cube faces black.

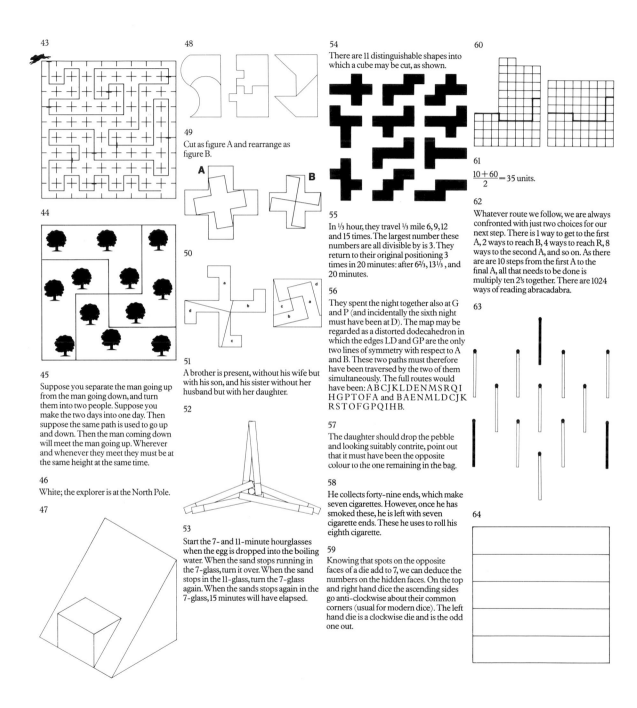

43

44

45

Suppose you separate the man going up from the man going down, and turn them into two people. Suppose you make the two days into one day. Then suppose the same path is used to go up and down. Then the man coming down will meet the man going up. Wherever and whenever they meet they must be at the same height at the same time.

46

White; the explorer is at the North Pole.

47

48

49

Cut as figure A and rearrange as figure B.

A   **B**

50

a
d   d
    b   c   a
    b
c

51

A brother is present, without his wife but with his son, and his sister without her husband but with her daughter.

52

53

Start the 7- and 11-minute hourglasses when the egg is dropped into the boiling water. When the sand stops running in the 7-glass, turn it over. When the sand stops in the 11-glass, turn the 7-glass again. When the sands stops again in the 7-glass, 15 minutes will have elapsed.

54

There are 11 distinguishable shapes into which a cube may be cut, as shown.

55

In ⅓ hour, they travel ⅓ mile 6, 9, 12 and 15 times. The largest number these numbers are all divisible by is 3. They return to their original positioning 3 times in 20 minutes: after 6⅔, 13⅓ , and 20 minutes.

56

They spent the night together also at G and P (and incidentally the sixth night must have been at D). The map may be regarded as a distorted dodecahedron in which the edges LD and GP are the only two lines of symmetry with respect to A and B. These two paths must therefore have been traversed by the two of them simultaneously. The full routes would have been: A B C J K L D E N M S R Q I H G P T O F A and B A E N M L D C J K R S T O F G P Q I H B.

57

The daughter should drop the pebble and looking suitably contrite, point out that it must have been the opposite colour to the one remaining in the bag.

58

He collects forty-nine ends, which make seven cigarettes. However, once he has smoked these, he is left with seven cigarette ends. These he uses to roll his eighth cigarette.

59

Knowing that spots on the opposite faces of a die add to 7, we can deduce the numbers on the hidden faces. On the top and right hand dice the ascending sides go anti-clockwise about their common corners (usual for modern dice). The left hand die is a clockwise die and is the odd one out.

60

61

$\frac{10+60}{2} = 35$ units.

62

Whatever route we follow, we are always confronted with just two choices for our next step. There is 1 way to get to the first A, 2 ways to reach B, 4 ways to reach R, 8 ways to reach the second A, and so on. As there are 10 steps from the first A to the final A, all that needs to be done is multiply ten 2's together. There are 1024 ways of reading abracadabra.

63

64

65

Imagine that everyone sits in a circle. One cuts a slice. He passes it to the person on his right, who may take it if he wishes. If not, he passes to his right, and so on round the circle. If no one has taken it by the time it returns to the person who cut it, he gets it. Whichever person ends up with the slice quits the circle. Any other person then cuts a new slice, and the process is repeated until the entire cake has been divided.

66

The pie can be cut into 22 pieces.

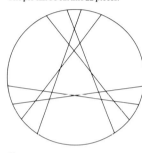

67

If you hold a cube so that one corner points directly towards you, the edges outline a hexagon; you will see that there is ample space for a square hole that can be slightly larger than the face of the cube itself.

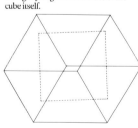

68

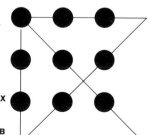

69

The ladder rises with the barge, so the water never reaches the bottom rung.

70

198 days. Every day it increased its height by one half of its original height. In 198 days, it reproduced its height 99 times and was therefore 100 times its original height.

71

Loop B must be cut.

72

The only true knot is C.

73

It must be on or very close to the International Dateline in the Pacific. When it is Sunday locally, on the other side of the line it will be either Saturday or Monday. In fact, the Solomon Islands is the only island group so positioned.

74

Fold a postcard in half. Cut along the fold so you are left with two equal halves. Take one half, fold in half again, and then cut at a slant. Take the other half and do the same but at a different degree of slant. The two pieces of each half appear quite different but are actually equal in area. As long as the slanted cuts begin and end at an equal distance from the top and bottom edge of the card, the two pieces must be equal in area.

75

Columbus died in 1506 whilst the telescope was not invented until 1609.

76

Martin should receive the red envelope containing the green card, and Michael the blue envelope which contains the red card. Mark should get the yellow envelope, which contains the blue card, and Matthew the green envelope which contains the yellow card.

77

There are six ways to reach the opposite corner of the roof, each taking four moves. You have five opportunities to make your first downward move: either

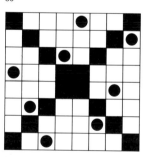

78

before starting or after any horizontal move. So the number of ways to reach point X is 30. There is just one route from X to B. By symmetry, there will be another 30 routes via each of Y and Z. So total possible routes = 30 x 3 = 90.

78

60 blocks remain. The complete pile would have been 6 x 6 x 4 = 144 half blocks (i.e. 72 whole blocks.) It can easily be visualised that 4 double blocks (each 2 x 2 x 1) would fill all but the top layer, and another two would complete that layer. So we need 6 double blocks. That means 12 ordinary blocks are missing from the original 72.

79

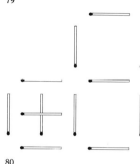

80

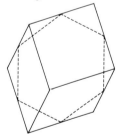

81

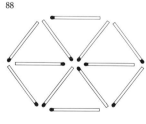

82

Two, leaving some areas of white.

83

Invert the Ace and the 8.

84

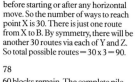

85

Since the pilot must be able to go in any direction from Buenos Aires without going out of his way, he could only be going to the antipodal point, that is, the point opposite Buenos Aires on the globe, which is Peking, China.

86

If the oarsman rows away from the cap for ten minutes it will take him another ten minutes to return to it. (The current is irrelevant: it acts equally on the cap and the boat.) In twenty minutes the river has carried the cap one mile. So its speed is three miles per hour.

87

The cut surface will have the outline shape of a regular hexagon. This may at first seem surprising as the hexagon seems to belong to the equilateral triangle group of figures and not to the right-angle group at all. In fact, the cut goes through all six faces of the cube and so the resulting outline has six sides.

88

89

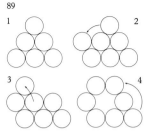

90

The safe combinations to leave are 7–4, 5–3 or 2–1. Start by taking one button from the pile holding 8.

91

If you plot out all the games it can be very tedious. But if instead of being interested in the winner, you decide to become interested in all the losers, the problem becomes much easier. Since there is but one winner there must be sixty-seven losers. Since each match has a loser, there will be just sixty-seven matches.

92

It can be both a square and a triangle. Fold right for a square, left for a triangle.

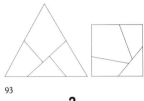

93

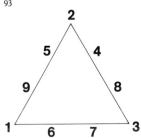

94

There are 31 different equilateral triangles and the design can be drawn in one continuous line with 16 turns.

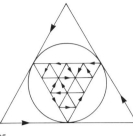

95

Begin with a layout of tail, head, tail. To get three heads up, turn over coins 1 and 2, 1 and 3, and 1 and 2.

96

The winning strategy is to remove one paperclip from the row that has six. The player who does this can control play so that the opponent is forced to pick up the last paperclip. On each subsequent turn, if your opponent's move leaves three non-empty heaps, play to keep the two larger ones unequal by one. But if he takes the singleton, play to keep the two remaining heaps equal. Sooner or later you will be able to make a winning move leaving either 1 or 3 clips.

97

The same 'impossible object' from a slightly different angle.

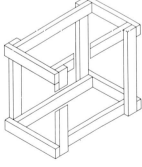

98

Yes. Follow these instructions carefully. The separate stages correspond numerically with the illustrations.

i   Fold all four corners into the centre.
ii   Then fold AB forward along the dotted line to meet DC.
iii Fold BF across to meet AE.
iv   Fold FG forward to meet BH.
v   Fold GJ across to meet FI.
vi   Cut straight through the bundle now obtained from corner to corner along the diagonal line, taking care that no squares of one colour fall accidentally on squares of the other.

The result: a cloth neatly separated into red and white squares.

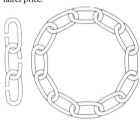

99

To make the bracelet without cutting more than three links, open all three links of one piece. Then use those three links to join the other three links into a circle. Thirty dollars would have been a fairer price.

100

The first and fourth chains match. The first will have the same pattern visible as the fourth, if you turn it upside down and rotate it 180 degrees.

101

The answer is simple. Because every handshake involves two people.

102

Ten people. Each shakes hands with nine others: each handshake is shared by two people.

103

One of the possible solutions:

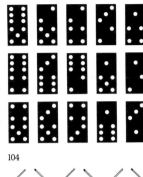

104

105

106

Consider the seating around the table as being around a circle. Your colleague does the first firing and you can break the circle at the opposite point to leave two exactly equal segments. You then simply follow exactly what he does but on the opposite segment. When you near the end if two people are left in each segment and your colleague removes his two you simply remove one of yours leaving him the last man to sack. If, however, he removes only one of his then you remove both of yours, thereby still leaving him the last man to sack.

107

Move both your hands towards your partner, separating the strings. Make an un-twisted loop in your string, tuck the loop through the string around your friend's right wrist, towards the fingers. Pass the loop over their fist and tuck it back through the string on the other side and you're free.

108

He loosens the centre loop so that the ring can be pushed up through it. He holds the ring against the front side of the panel while he seizes the double cord where it emerges from the centre hole. He pulls the double cord towards him dragging a double loop out of the central hole, and passes the ring through this double loop. He then reaches behind the panel and pulls the double loop back through the hole so that the cord is restored to starting position. The prisoner then only needs to slide the ring down through the centre loop to reach the knot at the far end, untie it, and escape.

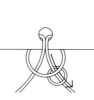

109

Let us tabulate the descriptions:

	Hair	Height	Shirt	Glasses
Cabby	Fair	Small	Blue	Yes
Warden	Dark	Average	Blue	Yes
Driver	Red	Tall	White	Yes
Worker	Bald	Small	Blue	No

Only one witness can be right about any detail, or there would have to be another detail that another witness is right about. Therefore, the driver did not wear glasses. The workman was right about that and thus wrong about everything else, so the driver did wear a white shirt, was not small or bald. The only detail the cabby can have right is the hair, therefore the driver must have been of average height.

110

The easiest solution is to stop looking at the problem as a triangle and instead look at it as a rosette of billiard balls with three extra points. If the extra points are moved around to the next position, the triangle is automatically reversed, in three moves.

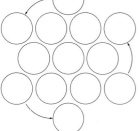

111

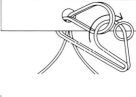

112

The missing number is 3. The number in each area denotes the number of bordering areas.

113

Odd numbers can be shown as a pyramid of squares and adding the next odd number will simply add a row to the bottom of the pile. However large this pile, you can always split it into two as shown. The two halves obtained fit together to give a square.

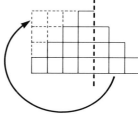

114

This is probably one of the longest palindromes (reads the same backwards) in the English language.

115

116

The circle and star can be transposed in seventeen moves. 1 circle. 2 star. 3 square. 4 circle. 5 triangle. 6 diamond. 7 circle. 8 square. 9 star. 10 triangle. 11 square. 12 circle. 13 diamond. 14 square. 15 triangle. 16 star. 17 circle.

117

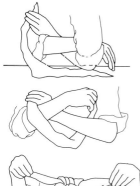

118

Twenty-seven hexagons.

119

First he takes Ann, and then returns to fetch Andrew. He takes Ann back again and leaves her on the first bank while he carries Mark across. Then he returns and fetches Ann.

120

Neither. Whatever decrees issued the ratio of boys to girls born is unchanged. Whoever the next mother in the country to give birth is, she always has a 50-50 chance of boy or girl.

121

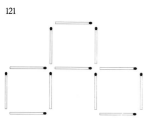

122

123

All the farmers need to do is tilt the barrel. As simple as that? If the edge of the surface of the ale touches the lip of the barrel at the same time that it touches the edge of the bottom of the barrel, then it must be half full (or half empty).

124

125

The diagram illustrates how the wood should be cut in two pieces to form the square table top. A, B, C, D are the corners. The way in which the piece E fits into the piece F will be obvious to the eye of the reader. The shaded part is the wood that is discarded.

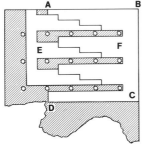

126

18, 446, 744, 073, 709, 551, 615 counters.

127

First move 2 and 3 to the extreme end; then fill the gap with 5 and 6. Fill the gap with 8 and 2; then finish with 1 and 5.

128

The four divisions are all areas of similar shape and size.

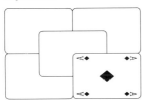

129

Both pencils are exactly the same length.

130

When the pieces fall apart, there would not be two pieces as one might expect, but still only one with an additional twist.

131

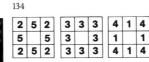

132

Fifteen can be counted in each direction.

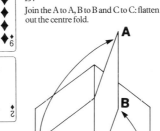

133

The first tramp drinks in sips. After each sip he replaces the stopper, puts his two thumbs at either end of the level of wine and inverts the bottle. When he has drunk exactly half the wine, the level in both upright and inverted positions will be exactly marked by his thumbs – thus indicating that the amount now missing from the bottle is exactly equal to the amount still there.

134

2	5	2		3	3	3		4	1	4
5		5		3		3		1		1
2	5	2		3	3	3		4	1	4

135

136

The first and second die yield thirty-six possible combinations. Of these, four (4–1, 3–2, 2–3 and 1–4) total 5; five (6– 2, 5–3, 4–4, 3–5 and 2–6) total 8; and three (6–4, 5–5 and 4–6) total 10. Park Lane would be the best choice for your hotel, as your opponent has a 5:36 chance of landing on that property.

137

Join the A to A, B to B and C to C: flatten out the centre fold.

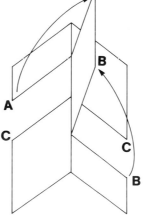

138

The first sheet is folded as follows. Hold it face down so that when you look down on it the numbered squares are in the position shown in the question.
Fold the right half on the left so that 5 goes on 2, 6 on 3, 4 on 1, and 7 on 8. Fold the bottom half up so that 4 goes on 5,

and 7 on 6. Now tuck 4 and 5 between 6 and 3, and fold 1 and 2 under the packet. Trim the pages, staple through the centre fold with page 4 on your left and page 5 on the right, and the eight page numbers will be in correct sequence.

139

The measures are equal.

140

All three know there are either two or three bowlers (if there was only one, only two hands would have gone up). Therefore there is either one top hat or none. If any one could see a top hat he would know he was wearing a bowler. Since no one has said anything they must all be wearing bowlers.

141

Looking at the problem, we can see from D that the apex of the black triangle must point towards the black square, so sections A and B must be fitted together as shown. By orienting such a cube to match the five pictures in the problem, we can read off the top symbol of each. The top symbol in each case is: A, white circle; B, black circle; C, white circle; D, white triangle; E, black triangle.

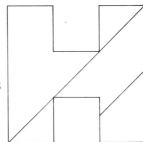

142

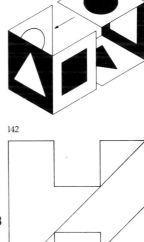

143

Since they weren't born of woman, neither Adam nor Eve had navels!

144

He is 52. She is 39.

145

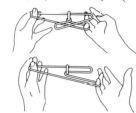

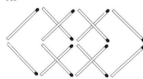

146

The letter L.

147

Seven. Red by itself, green by itself, yellow by itself, red and green, red and yellow, yellow and green, red and green and yellow.

148

149

The best approach is to select moves in short chains. Thus, after exchanging pieces 1 and 7, move piece 7 into position 7 (where piece 20 is), then move piece 20 into position 20 (where piece 16 is), and so on. On the sixth move, the exchange puts both pieces in the correct

square, so start a new chain. The quickest solution is 19 moves in 5 chains: 1–7, 7–20, 20–16, 16–11, 11–2, 2–24; 3–10, 10–23, 23–14, 14–18, 18–5; 4–19, 19–9, 9–22; 6–12, 12–15, 15–13, 13–25; 17–21.

150

Instead of drawing each route from A to C, it is simpler to solve the problem for points near A and progress point by point to C. The diagram labels all the points from 1a (which is A) to 5e (which is C). It is evident that there is only 1 route each from A to the nearest points on AB and AD (2a and 1b). You can get to 2b through either of these points (2 routes). Now the crossing 2c can be reached from 2b (2 routes) or from 1c (one more route, making 3 in all). Analogously, there are 3 routes to 3b. It becomes clear that the number of routes shown in each crossing is the sum of the number of routes shown immediately to the left and immediately below – which is logical, because all moves are up or to the right. Continue adding, working from point to point, until you reach C with its 70 different routes from A.

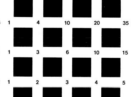

151

You should choose to go second. Imagine a flagpole planted in the centre of the site. After each of your opponent's turns, simply buy the corresponding plot or plots on the opposite side of the flagpole. This strategy places you in a position to purchase the last plot.

152

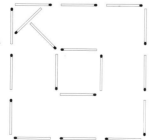

153

There must be 6 entrants who run 100 metres and 200 metres but not 400 metres. (We can also deduce that there are 42 competitors altogether including 9 who only wish to run 400 metres and 3 who do all three distances.)

154

The jockeys exchange horses.

155

The ball would travel 100 metres.
$$
\begin{aligned}
& \quad 90 \text{ metres} \\
+ & \quad\ \ 9 \text{ metres} \\
+ & \quad\ \ 0.9 \text{ metres} \\
+ & \quad\ \ 0.09 \text{ metres} \dots \dots \\
= & \ 100 \text{ metres total, after a (theoretically)}
\end{aligned}
$$
infinite number of bounces.

156

512: hexagons contain the square of the preceding number; circles contain half the preceding number.

157

Turn left at each crossroads.

158

He asks either man: 'If I asked your companion the way, what would he say?' Then he takes the opposite fork to the one indicated.

159

Three moves.

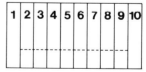

160

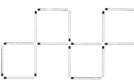

161

This is a very rich investigation with many possibilities. The rule is that two circles of the same colour have a white circle below and between them; two different circles have a black one. Note that we consider the left edge of the pattern to be adjacent to the right, as if the dots were inscribed on the surface of a cylinder.

Since only a finite number of seven-dot combinations are possible, any such pattern is bound to repeat eventually. As it so happens, this one does after just two more lines.

162

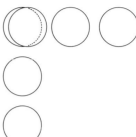

163

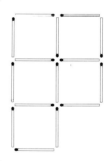

164

The bookworm travelled sixteen inches. As you can see when looking at the books the cover of volume 1 is on the right, the back of volume 10 on the left.

1	2	3	4	5	6	7	8	9	10

165

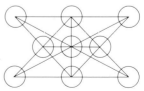

166

This route takes the zookeeper past all the cages.

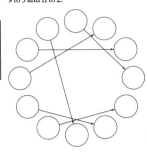

167

It only seems impossible to separate the pieces because we assume that the joint must run at right angles to the edge of the block. If the joints run diagonally then the top and bottom blocks can be easily slid apart.

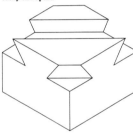

168

The total number of faces is 27 x 6 = 162. The number of gold faces is 6 x 9 = 54. The chance of a gold face is $^{54}/_{162}$ or 1 in 3.

169

Turn the problem page upside-down.

170

I am my own grandfather.

171

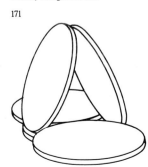

172

Move 12 to 3, 7 to 4, 10 to 6 (7 has left a gap) 8 to 1 (12 and 10 have left a gap), 9 to 5 and 11 to 2.

173

One method is to start by cutting a thin spiral round and round until you reach the centre. You are now left with a long strip of paper which does not fit the conditions since no joins are allowed. But all you then have to do is to cut down the centre of this strip stopping short of the edge at the beginning and the end.

174

He must pick up 7 shirts to tide him over until the following Monday. Hence he must deposit 7 shirts each Monday. Counting the shirt he wears on Monday, the required total is 15. (Note that he cannot get by with only 14 by swapping his Monday shirt for a clean one and turning it in to the laundry, as he will be caught short the following Monday.)

175

No. The down-draft from the ducks' wings will exactly balance their weight. You can't avoid Newton's first law: action and reaction are equal and opposite.

176

Yes, if they use the following sequence:

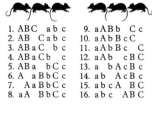

1. A B C a b c		9. a A B b C c
2. A B C a b c		10. a A b B c C
3. A B a C b c		11. a A b B c C
4. A B a C b c		12. a A b c B C
5. A B a b C c		13. a b A c B c
6. A a B b C c		14. a b A c B c
7. A a B b C c		15. a b c A B C
8. a A B b C c		16. a b c A B C

177

One way of looking at it is: the dealer bought the painting for $70 and sold it for $80: profit $10. But then he bought it back for $90 having just sold it for $80: he loses $10. Thus far his profit is nil. By applying the same faulty reasoning, he then sells it for $100 after buying the painting back for $90: so he's made another $10. Overall profit: $10.
Another misleading argument runs like this: he sells for $80 after buying for $70: profit $10. Then he loses $20 by buying back for $90 what he originally paid $70 for. But he gains $10 by selling for $100 what he had bought back for $90. Result: he breaks even.
Neither argument is correct. Both involve the use of the same sums of money twice. The simplest way to view it is perhaps this: his total outlay is $70 + $90 or $160. But his payments amount to $80 + $100 or $180.
Overall profit: $20.

178

Taking the sentence one clause at a time:
The one you did after the one you did before this one is this one.
In other words:
'…the puzzle you solved after you solved the puzzle you solved before you solved this one' is this one.
Hence the question may be rephrased this way: 'If the puzzle you solved before this one was harder than this one, was the puzzle you solved before this one harder than this one?'
Obviously the answer to the question is just yes.